LEARNING TO SEE
A Matter of Light

LEARNING TO SEE
A Matter of Light

by
Howard M. Brandston
LC, FIES, Hon. CIBSE,
FIALD, PLDA, MSLL

Published by the Illuminating Engineering Society of North America
© 2008 the Illuminating Engineering Society of North America
All rights reserved

Printed in the United States of America

Reproduction or translation of any part of this work beyond that permitted by Section 107 or 108 of the United States Copyright Act of 1976, without the prior written consent of the publisher, is unlawful. No part of this book whether in hardcopy or electronic form may be reproduced, distributed, posted or otherwise made available beyond original distribution means in any form or by any means or stored in a database or retrieval system. Requests for permission or further information should be addressed to the Illuminating Engineering Society of North America.

ISBN – 13: 978-0-87995-225-9

Library of Congress Control Number: 2008926614

Interior book design by Robert Vizzini,
Vizzini Design & Photography, New York, New York

Praise for
LEARNING TO SEE: A Matter of Light

Howard Brandston has written a book that meets all the criteria for one that you won't want to put down. It is filled with interesting information in an "Oh, that's why that happens" way. It is entertaining but not frivolous. It forces critical thinking but is easy to digest. It teaches without being condescending. It is sophisticated but not intimidating. It is challenging but accessible ... He has also shared with us his remarkable career. It has been filled with important responsibilities (how the Statue of Liberty should be perceived) and dedicated to enhancing people's enjoyment (how the Erie Canal is experienced) and understanding the world around us (presenting our past at the Museum of Natural History) ... For those of us who have always taken it for granted, Howard Brandston has put light in a whole new light.

—Dan Ciampa, business consultant and author of
Taking Advice: How Leaders Get Good Counsel and Use it Wisely

Acknowledgments

For everyone's information, I am not solely responsible for writing this book. I had mused about writing one for decades, but it was the constant prodding and encouragement by my wife, Melanie, that kept the notion in my head. She was not alone. Watching my friends Peter Boyce, Derek Phillips and Kit Cuttle produce great works further inspired me to add my voice to the literature of lighting. And other colleagues encouraged me as well—Philip Gabriel, Hayden McKay, Robert Prouse and many others.

From the basement and shelves full of countless articles, position papers, design reports and other literature that I had written over the years and the miscellaneous other documents I accumulated, I thought surely there must be a book. Patricia Rizzo, a remarkable former student of mine, sorted through the morass and played the major role in organizing it into a format that made sense. Without her patience and diligence, there would be no book, and I will be forever grateful to her.

This book, which is a series of related but independent essays, needed something more to make it a cohesive readable treatise; another person to whom I am most grateful is my editor, Craig DiLouie, who did wonders in pulling it all together into a comprehensible volume.

This book is dedicated to my wife, Melanie, whose gentle but unceasing prodding to write a book prevailed. Without her perseverance, I would probably never have been able to sustain the effort required to write this book. And to my children: Perry, Raj, Lori and Sarah, including my grandchildren: Melody, Ted, Julia and Daniel; they comprise a family that illuminates my life. And to my brother, Andrew Brandston.

"The question is not what you look at, but what you see."
—*Henry David Thoreau*

CONTENTS

Preface 3
Foreword 5
Introduction 9
Learning to See 17
  1 Shades of Light 19
  2 Sight: When the Orb Blinks 21
  3 Getting to Know Light 27
  4 Learning to See 33
Taking Responsibility 37
  5 Curiosity and Skepticism 39
  6 The Horse's Mouth 43
Getting Creative 47
  7 Conjuring up the Image 49
  8 Subconscious to Conscious 51
  9 Space: Substructure of a Greater Whole 55
  10 A Sense of Place 59
  11 Two Points of View 71
Communication 75
  12 Designing with Light 77
  13 Write It Down 85
  14 Lighting the Lady 89
  15 Illuminating History, Education and Ceremony 99
  16 A Grand Vision for Detroit 107
  17 Learning to See: An Emotional Response 113
Appendices 117
  Appendix I Explanations of Popular Lighting Terms 119
  Appendix II Ethics and Design 129
  Appendix III Wit and Wisdom 133
  About Howard Brandston 137

Preface

The time has come for me to write this book, not for myself, but because no book exists today that truly covers the art of lighting design in the context of life. Nor do the books on lighting design talk about light and lighting in the language of ordinary people—the folks who use the light. They should be given the opportunity to understand light and its application, lighting.

So this book is written for professionals in the design fields and, in general, the educated person. The design professional will gain insights into how to use light, expand his or her worldview and use creativity and open-mindedness to excel at everything he or she undertakes. The educated person will gain insights into how light impacts his or her daily life and how to use it to enhance quality of life. After all, there are more "lighting designers" in this country than any other profession—people lighting their own homes.

Many books offer lighting design parameters and most provide solid coverage of all the technical components that surround light and lighting. But is that enough? It is like teaching a surgeon how to most effectively use scalpels and clamps but not teach him anatomy and physiology. That anatomy and physiology of life in the built environment will serve as a philosophical model for any contribution this book might make to the literature on light and lighting. The basic purpose of light and its application will be presented within a holistic context—life itself.

I have never worked within the shackles of rules, recommendations and calculations. Rather, I circumvent these methods and defer to real experiences worthy of influencing my decisions in life and my designs. Inspired by scientists and sages on the subject of physics, vision, art and the humanities, I have lived and practiced by my senses, constantly seeing, touching and probing. Ask any of my students—rarely a class would pass when I didn't tug on someone's shirt sleeve and prod a question, or chuckle and say, "This, this is what you need to think about." Critiques in my design studios would sometimes result in tears, or at least looks of devastation, because I would ask the hard questions. I wouldn't let them escape with a rote response or an ordinary solution. If they did come up with such a response or solution, it was because they didn't allow themselves to "see," didn't give themselves permission to use all their senses, or their sense, to really hit a homerun—to understand the problem so well that an extraordinary solution would have come naturally. So I poked, I tugged, I pleaded with them to poke back. Some learned to think, while some continued to rely on formulae and fear. My hope is that now, years later, as they consider a problem, any problem in their lives, they may, all of a sudden, feel my tug, smile, and realize the point I was trying to drive home. But even those who never subscribed to my repeated prodding cannot deny my signature utterance, "What is it you wish to see?"

Words I live by. *A phrase that deceives in its simplicity.*

The following pages, the expression of a successful philosophy and career in lighting design, should reveal why.

Foreword

Parts of this book will be more easily understood by some audiences, parts by others. Keep reading—you will understand again.

It is a pity they don't teach wonder in school, that most genuine of qualities possessed by children yet absent in many adults who are too often jaded by the stresses of life. Our daily adventures should be rife with awe, a conclave of wonders. If nothing else, this book seeks to ignite a little spark of wonder, to awaken a curiosity for the acquisition of knowledge through an awareness of light and lighting. We recognize, perceive and understand stimuli. Yet how do we manage and express what we've seen? These pages employ lighting, the application of light, merely as an approach to kindle the skill of "learning to see," lest we waste a rare gift. It seeks to encourage confidence in our acceptance of what we see.

When Prometheus handed us the gift of divine fire in our dark caves, fire he had stolen from Zeus, it was as if he were giving us an Aladdin's lamp—a gift of pure magic, empowering us to see anything we wished to see and more. Inventiveness, productivity and respect for the immortal gods abounded; culture rapidly developed. Yet we mortals have used little of the essence of that gift, have taken little advantage of the power that light yields—the magnitude of which appears to have been barely realized. Even in the world of science, light is a paradox—while sound waves need air, and water waves need water, light waves can travel in a vacuum. But humans do not live in a vacuum—we interact, we touch, we feel, we taste and, if we are fortunate, we see without effort—a natural sensation. Do we realize, though, how we see, what gears must turn and what systems must link in order to register what our eyes absorb?

What each of us sees is not simply the result of a processing mechanism, but rather it is that thing embedded in our brain, that vision that our mind constructs, drawn from a memory recorded, a sensation felt, an aroma detected—it is complex, sometimes indefinable—but it translates into what we see. A comprehensive system, comprised of physiological, psychological, cognitive and emotional components, stokes perception.

In the world of science there are people who can see without any data; then there are others who can't see until they have the data. Both are valuable—for you can know something, but if science proves it, you can objectively know it. It is necessary to balance the subjectivity that identifies the world of art—creates that important bit of tension that elevates the standards of the two worlds. There is a vast body of knowledge about the eye, the brain, the seeing processes, including an appreciation of the gift of sight. Legendary people such as Louis Bell, Peter Boyce, Richard Gregory, Edwin Land, Mark Rea, Oliver Sacks and Semir Zeki* have contributed to this great body of knowledge—to the entire process of how you see.

In the early 18th century, Sir Isaac Newton initiated the scientific study of color vision, further developed by Young, then Helmholtz in the early 19th century. How many of us

---

*
Louis Bell – editor, educator, engineer, inventor; founding member of IESNA
Peter Boyce – research scientist, teacher, author
Richard Gregory – neuropsychologist, author, expert on visual perception
Edwin Land – inventor of the Polaroid camera; developed the Retinex Theory, which states that humans recognize colors even though they appear different under different types of illumination, called color constancy
Mark Rea – research scientist, educator; director of RPI's Lighting Research Center
Oliver Sacks – neurologist, author; dubbed the 'poet laureate' of medicine by The New York Times
Semir Zeki – cognitive neuroscientist, specializing in 'visual brain' research

know that color—that seemingly simple yet most complex of phenomena—evolved due to some evolutionary purpose to help us recognize which pieces of the world belong together?

The ability to assess light will benefit all in some way, both those who love light and those who are only mildly aware of it, even if simply relighting your garage or office. When you walk into a room you should query, "If I could change one thing about this space, what would it be?" If that doesn't achieve the desired results, move on to the next item on the list. The excitement derives from the experience being so individual, so subjective. What one person sees that needs changing will be entirely different from what another sees. "There is an inevitable divergence, attributable to the imperfections of the human mind, between the world as it is and world as men perceive it." (James William Fulbright, Speech in the Senate; 27 March 1964)

When finished reading this, you may come away with a self-confidence born of an understanding of what you see, and the courage to think for yourself.

Introduction

Design implies purpose and intent. We have all heard the expression, "to do something by design." The Oxford Dictionary defines a designer as someone who originates a plan or scheme. Are we not then, each and every one of us, designers in and of this life? We design the minutes of our days, the days of our weeks; we design our cars, our homes, our wardrobes, our landscapes. We express our personalities by the colors we wear, the fabrics with which we dress our windows, the twist of the tree trunks that frame our property, even the spokes that spin our wheels. How we design our lives creates an image that is perceived, and often judged, by others. We can fine-tune that image by considering four elements that are integral to executing our designs: *learning to see, taking responsibility, creativity* and *communication*. When all is said and done, it is the plaiting of these four elements that will guide us back to the art of thinking, a kind of wake-up jolt forcing us to take inventory of our lives and ask, "Where am I, where am I going, how am I getting there and am I contributing anything worth anything?"

Learning to see

"By subtle use of light, and without altering so much as a word of the dramatist's text, it is possible sometimes to change completely the impression a whole scene conveys."

—*Theatre Lighting* by Louis Hartmann

My roots in lighting began in the theater in the New York of the 1950s, with perhaps the greatest mentor to grace the field of lighting, Stanley McCandless (1897-1967). Edison's commercial lamp had only been in existence for 18 years at the time of McCandless's birth; by the time he passed away, almost every light source we have today had already been developed, from discharge lamps to light-emitting diodes (LEDs). You could say McCandless grew with the lighting industry or, just maybe, the industry grew with him. He embraced the science and converted it to art through stage, theater and architecture. You see, what lighting artists knew back then came from everyday experience and pure emotion. People who started in theater lighting were not bound by rules and calculations. They had to figure out ways of communicating the emotion of the actors or performers or of the scene itself. The technical aspects were just the tools they used to portray the emotions they wished the audience to see.

The simplest defining characteristic of lighting, yet perhaps its greatest mystery, is "the process of learning to see." Learning to see means a mental notation of the causes of our emotions or reactions in response to the experience of the scene we are viewing. It is essential that one be able to see what one looks at—to appreciate, to remember, to record. To understand any given visual scene and the emotion it evokes, one must do more than just look. One must understand the context in life into which it fits, the influence of culture, the importance of demographics, and the human response to scale. Context, culture, demographics, scale—these are essential to understanding how people respond to space, but are not (nor can they be) taught in standard practice.

You can't think about something you know nothing about. You have to be literate—some people even write those feelings down. A musician thinks about music and writes it down. Some people develop a method of "writing lighting." Those people have truly learned to see.

This process of building a databank of memories of lighted environments from real life experience—a databank of real knowledge which can serve in any capacity as we design our lives—is fundamental to learning to see.

Taking responsibility
  "A foolish faith in authority is the first enemy of truth."
  —Albert Einstein

The raw truth of what it means to take responsibility is echoed in the words of 18th century playwright Richard Brinsley Sheridan, who said, "The burden on the university is to increase the number of those who are willing to undergo the fatigue of judging for themselves." To be accountable, to take responsibility both personally and professionally, we must first be accountable to ourselves—this precludes any laziness or shirking of conscience. A daily maintenance of ethics, if you will.

Personally, do we bear the burden of gaining more knowledge with each new experience? Are we perpetually learning to see—intellectually, artistically, emotionally and physically—to add to our memory and sensory database? As designers of life, we are responsible for the quality of our life, for our enjoyment. We are responsible for providing creativity—for delivering unique solutions to ourselves, our colleagues and our clients. How well we perform will expand our relationships. A simple metric would be to ask ourselves, "Have I seen it before? Is there a benefit to doing something new and creative?"

Professionally, we form relationships with people; we are responsible for clearly communicating our vision to them and, ultimately, for using those lessons to make our clients happy. When building, know the codes, rules and recommended practices so well to be able to decide when *not to be bound* by them. Just think: The keys on a piano are in the same order starting from middle "C," regardless of whether it is an upright, grand or organ. Whatever the instrument, every musician faces the same configuration of notes. Some laws are immutable. Some musicians are creative.

The fugues of Bach are a perfect illustration of what I mean. Now the fugue is the most rigid, narrowly defined of musical forms. Yet within those parameters, Bach produced a magnificent body of music. He wrote law-abiding fugues in every key, major and minor, as if to show what could be done within the form. He was at the same time true to the rules of his craft and true to his genius. Bach was accountable.

Never have I felt more accountable than back in the mid 1980s, when I was presented with one of the most exciting projects of my career—I speak of the commission to create new lighting for a remarkable woman on the occasion of her hundredth birthday. The lady in question had green skin, wore spikes in her hair and measured over thirty meters from head to toe. You know her as the Statue of Liberty. It was an enormous challenge and I felt both honored and humbled to be granted it. Above all, I felt accountable.

I was accountable to the French-American Committee for the Statue of Liberty and the architects, the group that commissioned me. I felt enormously accountable to the great lady herself. And finally, I was accountable to the entire population of the United States—all 250 million of them, and millions of other people around the world who admire her for the freedoms she represents. Bearing responsibility yields great rewards. *continued on page 14*

Figure i-1. ... From imagination to reality.
© JEFF GOLDBERG/ESTO. ALL RIGHTS RESERVED.

Lighting design is a series of planned experiences involving people and space. Put people in all your sketches—they might remind you to think about lighting them.

In 1995, I attended an evening of poetry and essay readings presented by formerly illiterate adults learning to read and write at The Literacy Volunteers of New York City (LVNYC). I listened to poets and essayists, to the creations that came from the minds of people that did not possess the tools most of us have—the ability to read, write, speak well, solve problems, communicate, analyze, debate. But you know, when those people read their work, they had something that transcended those tools—they had thoughtful, meaningful, wonderful ideas. And they expressed them with an emotion that was so moving it was hard to measure. They did not write with perfect grammar nor speak with perfect diction, but their messages reached out with a perfection that communicated their experiences. Their words also made clear the frustration of what it was like to have all that creativity bottled up through half their adult lives, choked for the lack of tools. These are people who, for perhaps 25 to 40 years, have amazingly conducted their lives as employees, parents and even entrepreneurs while lacking the skills to be able to read a street sign or a newspaper headline. Tears came to my eyes: tears of joy for them.

Lacking the tools that we—the privileged, the educated—have at our disposal at all times, these new authors were able to release what was in their minds by using the communication tool that they knew best: pure emotion.

By drawing, speaking and writing our ideas, we increase our chances of communicating clearly. Braiding the elements one by one—*learning to see, taking responsibility, being creative, communicating clearly*—consequently knowing how to see, enables you to be more articulate in your communication, a quality that has a significant impact not only on the world's impression of you, but on your perception of yourself.

Creativity

"*Creative thinking may simply mean the realization that there's no particular virtue in doing things the way they have always been done.*"

—Rudolph Flesch

The greatest contribution a person can offer himself or his circle of friends is creativity and originality, even though this may entail a departure from conventional wisdom. In order to do that you must be loose. Lose your inhibitions. As I once told a student of mine who was shackled by her fear of drawing, "Your fingers are constipated—just draw, the paper's not going to bite you!" I, for one, think we labor under too many rules and restrictions, often self-imposed. When one only follows the rules, there is nothing to be held accountable for. *Rules are a substitute for thinking!*

What kind of life do you wish to lead? Whatever the circumstances—writing an essay, designing a theater or lighting a hospital, bridge or office tower, your own office or home—approach it as if you had never done anything like it before. As if *no one* had ever done anything like it before—because, in fact, no one has. No two of anything are identical. It therefore follows that no two evaluations or solutions can be the same.

As designers of your own life, isn't creativity a requirement? Do you bear the burden of original thinking? Once you think of each part of or each project in your life as a one-time-only puzzle, you've chosen the more difficult path; you've chosen originality over conformity. Let originality become your cloak. When you walk briskly through a crowd, you are purposeful, when you ascend an escalator you assimilate your surroundings, when your car is poised at a red light you peruse—people recognize you because your style is distinct. You are a constant observer, learning to see, perfecting your communication skills.

Would you aspire to less?

Communication

"The real voyage of discovery does not consist of seeking new landscapes but in having new eyes." —Marcel Proust

Each new project is one of discovery. A client once remarked to me, "This place looks exactly as you said it would." He recognized what I wished for him to see. Being able to see leads to an understanding, a comprehension so deep that it allows the release of the vision in your head, and perception then jumps to life; for how can you capture the mesmerizing blues and scarlets of a candle's flame in a drawing if the clear image is not vivid in your own mind? How can you describe the Tiffany glass chandelier over your "usual" table at the neighborhood bistro if you haven't paid attention to it once during your weekly Friday night visits?

Learning to See

1
Shades of Light

"Light, like music, fills, reveals and creates space."
—the author

LIGHT IS TIME'S SWIFTEST TRAVELER. Light allows us to see not only through our senses, but through our soul. It is a word that evokes a wide range of feelings within different people. To a philosopher, light is a metaphor for knowledge; to the scientist, it is a fundamental component of his or her work; and to the scenic artist, it is a tool to manipulate emotion. It has been defined by Maxwell and painted by Caravaggio. To the rest of us, who are sighted, it is the primary medium through which we acquire information. Light is energy—it is matter by which all life is measured.

A solitary, universal language unto itself, light is a link through all humanity, encompassing the entire spectrum of needs and emotions. It defines cultures and reveals architecture. It creates shadows and is born of shadow. Light has the power to uplift, soothe, enhance visibility and discrimination and generate a sense of comfort or even discomfort at times. Light can be harnessed to inspire, befriend, create a sense of community.

Indeed, we can mark the birth of civilization with the use of the first primitive oil lamp in the caves of Lascaux. By its light, our ancestors painted animal hunts and performed ritual songs and dances; in short, they passed on their lore, culture and learning to the next generation. In the glow of that first oil lamp, they found a source of beauty and discovered light's magic. They could prolong the day, banish the night and use the gift of newfound time in pursuit of learning and leisure and craft. Moreover, the conquest of light afforded them the safety and security so essential for an environment in which knowledge and art could flourish. By a lamp such as this, not only did great artists paint the caves, they also used light to keep the wolves away.

Light signifies the triumph of culture over ignorance, good over evil. "As far as we can discern," Karl Jung wrote, "the sole purpose of human existence is to kindle a light in the darkness of being." The *goodness* of light permeates our language. We learn, and become enlightened; we have a spiritual epiphany, and say that we have seen the light. We speak of the one we love as "the light of my life." How often do we allude to light as representative of *beginnings*—the Olympic torch; of *faith*—"Light is my armor," said St. Paul; of *freedom*—the torch of liberty; of *goodness*—an angel's halo; of *safety* and *survival*—lighthouses, headlights; of *soul*—the inner light; of *understanding*—to see the light. Light is everywhere. We see it with our eyes closed. We see it in our dreams.

Light gives rhythm to life through both visual and nonvisual effects. It regulates our days, our nights, our seasons, our body clocks.

Light enables us to see. Lighting design enables us to see what it is we wish to see.

2
Sight: When the Orb Blinks

"During all our waking hours we are deriving knowledge and pleasure from the exercise of sight."
—P.M. Harmon, *The Scientific Letters and Papers of James Clerk Maxwell*, Cambridge University Press, Cambridge, 1990, vol.1. p. 675

SEEING IS SUCH AN EASY AND NATURAL thing to do that, for the most part, it takes considerable discipline to realize that there are opportunities to enhance this ability. Seeing is partially a function of the eye and the camera is often used as a model to describe the eye. But the fascination really lies in their dissimilarities. The eye does not produce pictures in the brain. When we look at something, a pattern of neural activity represents the object, and to the brain, is the object. The eye and brain are continually processing information; a few minute cues are all that is required to attract attention and result in recognition.

Seeing utilizes many more sources of information than those meeting the eye. It includes knowledge gained from previous experience and usually relates to all our other senses such as touch, taste, smell, hearing. There is a stimulation and response—pain, caution, like, dislike. This process transcends experience and is the foundation of our knowledge without which our lives would be severely limited. This process is *perception*.

Perception is a dynamic searching for the best interpretation of the available data. The data is sensory information, and also knowledge of the other characteristics of objects observed. In simple terms, we must learn to see—most people just look. Perceiving and thinking are not independent. You must use your eyes and engage your brain to visually experience and truly interact with a space instead of merely looking at it.

What Mr. Maxwell, an English physicist ranked next to Newton in importance, is referring to is the potential of being able to see and gaining something from it. Our essential sight mechanism is, of course, the eye—the conduit of both direct and reflected energy sensation to the ultimate receiver of that sensation, the brain. Vision, man's most developed sense, depends on light. To see, we need light. Light is visually evaluated radiant energy. We have learned in the last hundred years that all so-called electromagnetic radiation is essentially the same. The difference between them is their frequency and only a very narrow band of these frequencies (less than an octave) stimulates vision.

A quantum is the smallest amount of radiant energy existing. The receptors of the retina are so sensitive they can be stimulated by a single quantum. It takes five to 10 quanta to experience a flash. A sailor on watch and adapted to darkness can, on a clear night, see the lighting of a cigarette about 15 miles away.

Depending on whose data or interpretations you accept, sight accounts for 76 to 90 percent of all external knowledge acquired by people with vision. Structurally, our eye is divided into optical and neurological components (Figure 2-1). The optical components, such as the cornea, crystalline lens, pupil and intraocular humors, produce tears, allow us to focus and actually transmit light; the neurological components, which include the retina and optic nerve, permit evaluation of the transmitted light.

Sight is initiated when photons, or particles of light, fall on the retina, which is a light-sensitive extension of the brain. It is that mesh-like layer at the rear of our eye that contains three layers of interconnected neural cells, each cell sensitive to intensity and color. One of these layers is composed of rod and cone cells, which derive their name from their respective shapes. These cells, which function as photoreceptors or light detectors, convert light into electrical pulses, which in turn stimulate a visual response in our brain (R.L. Gregory, 1997). Cones are color sensitive and are active in daylight or photopic conditions, while rods allow us to see black, white and shades of gray, and are active in darkness, or scotopic conditions. During dusk-like, or mesopic conditions, both rods and cones are active.

The three cone photoreceptors respond to short, medium and long wavelengths, known as S, M and L cones. Each responds primarily to one color in the spectrum, but responds to all colors to some degree. Color is the result of a series of calculations performed by the brain. The brain's visual cortex is divided into five sorting bins, so to speak, with different bins sorting out different information. The "bins" are connected but have different functions.

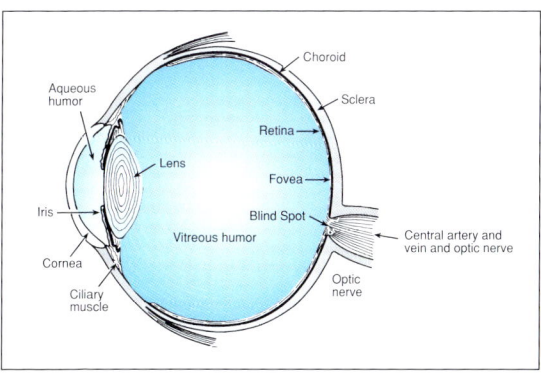

Figure 2-1: **A horizontal section through the eye. The approximate length from the cornea to the retina is 24mm. Only half the photons entering the eye reach our photoreceptors in the retina due to absorption and scattering of light within the lenses and transparent media of the eye (IESNA** *Lighting Handbook***, 9th Edition, 2000).**

In the realm of color, Isaac Newton, using a prism, found that white light could be split into all colors of the spectrum, which could then be recombined into white light when traveling through a second prism. In the 18th century, Thomas Young put forth the theory that a combination of red, green and blue can produce all colors, and believed that the eye determines what we see, not physics. Edwin Land, in 1960, repeated Young's color-mixing experiment using photographic transparencies and patterns rather than patches of light, and found that we are built to recognize the permanent properties of objects, not just the wavelengths reflected. Paradoxically, the color of an object must be constructed not just from wavelengths coming from the brain, but everything around it—cues from the world we live in. This creates a constancy.

Once we open our eyes, we're privy to a world of colors, textures, shapes and movements. Our eyes literally drink in these ingredients upside down and sideways, and then leave it to our brain to sort out the concoction. All of this happens with a time delay of 1/10 of a second, the time needed to integrate the intensity of light entering the eye. Think about it, there is an object in the vast openness of space, a word on this page for example, that somehow travels as a recognizable image to our mind. The brain lives in an ever-changing environment, yet selects constant, unchanging physical characteristics of objects from the ever-changing information it receives from these objects—separating itself from the fluctuations of constant change. This applies to senses in general since no object, surface or sound is seen or sensed in one condition exclusively. They are presented in varying contexts, multiple surroundings, different angles and distances, changing illumination conditions—and still they preserve their identity. While constancy is not unique to color vision, it is more easily understood in terms of it. Therefore, the color of a surface becomes a function of the brain, not the world outside (Semir Zeki, *A Vision of the Brain*).

A design definition of light would celebrate and unify light in its role as a giver and shaper of our lives—as a swift, infinite flow of energy that encompasses life itself. Light is a natural thing. I have never witnessed artificial or unnatural light. I have seen daylight, sunlight, gaslight, firelight, neon light and so on, and they are all real because we perceive them. That is because light *requires* a personal perceptual evaluation.

Light is transported by our eyes and visual system to be interpreted and evaluated in our brain, tempered by the experiences of our memories. We use light to discern size and shape of objects and to construct color. Consciously or not, we are perpetually evaluating light to navigate and communicate. It is the very finite portion of the electromagnetic spectrum that our visual system senses, defined as *visually evaluated radiant energy*. Definitions such as the following, however, are of little value as related to learning to see. When the Illuminating Engineering Society of North America (IESNA) states that light is, "For illuminating engineering purposes…radiant energy that is capable of stimulating the human retina and creating a visual sensation," and "defined in terms of its relative efficiency throughout the electromagnetic spectrum lying between 380 and 770 nanometers (nm)," what layperson could possibly know what that means? These definitions are both at once colorless and cultureless. They dissect human beings into their separate and disparate organisms, strip them of their heritage and individuality.

Just as we do not need a thermometer to tell us whether we are hot or cold, we certainly do not need a light meter to tell us whether or not we can see. I have never seen a light meter that had eyes, nor one that can measure emotion. At least a thermometer can confirm why we are hot or cold, but a light meter can't tell us very much about seeing, or how we feel—the things we really need to know. All the light meter can do is measure the radiant energy at the spot at which we are holding it. To emphasize once again: We are in a process of searching for what it is we wish to see, not the physiological process of how we are seeing it.

In innumerable ways, light excites our brain. But first we must blink.

3
Getting to Know Light

"Good lighting is defined at the beginning of each project with the client."   —the author

THERE IS A LITTLE INSTRUMENT that some lighting designers and other professionals use to train their eye to see—one that would aid anyone interested in discerning the behavior of light—the spectroscope. The spectroscope will show the spectral power distribution—more simply, the energy level distribution of each wavelength in the visible spectrum—of light sources in a space. In order to work with a medium such as light, you must first learn how it behaves; become familiar with it. Understand the impact that differences in the spectrum have on people. It is part of learning about the impact of the color of light. See why things look different in different lights. Wavelength behaves differently than pigment; combining wavelengths is an additive process. By overlapping the three primary colors of light—red, blue and green—one can produce white light as well as any color in the visible spectrum. Conversely, combining pigments is a subtractive process. When mixing paint colors together, or using a printer, pigments subtract or remove colors from white. Surfaces that do not emit light absorb colors. An apple, for example, absorbs all colors other than red, therefore we see whatever is left—red (R.L.Gregory).

In pigments or colorants, however, a primary color is defined as one that subtracts or absorbs a primary color of light and reflects or transmits the other two. So the primary colors in pigments (sometimes called subtractive primaries) are magenta, cyan and yellow—the secondary colors of light.

We see by contrast, and contrast varies with adaptation. In a multiple contrast mode, gray on black, gray on white, the gray on black looks brighter to the eye at a given intensity than the gray on white, because of simultaneous contrast; however, a luminance meter reads the gray at the same intensity whether it is against the black or against the white. Other unique and more complex contrasts are introduced when a variety of hues form the visual picture. It is further complicated by specific wavelengths which produce the sensation of color.

Guess, estimate, measure

The process of guessing, estimating and measuring is a fundamental methodology for learning about light and lighting until it becomes second nature.

Walk into a space. Do you like it or not? What do you notice first? What would you change if you could change one thing about it? This is *cognitively interacting* with the space.

How much light is there? What equipment is producing it? Look at the palm of your hand. Make a *guess*.

Now is time to *estimate*. Count the light fixtures and estimate the wattage in the room, then divide by the space's area to get the footcandles produced. Use the palm of your hand as a guide. In very low light levels, determine if there is enough light to see by attempting to read the serial numbers on a banknote.

Finally, *measure* light levels with a light meter. How did you do?

Over time, you'll surprise yourself with how much better you can evaluate light levels without the use of the meter.

Simple: your hand, a light meter, a banknote and a spectroscope. Guess, estimate, measure—these are the basic tools of a designer to learn about light.

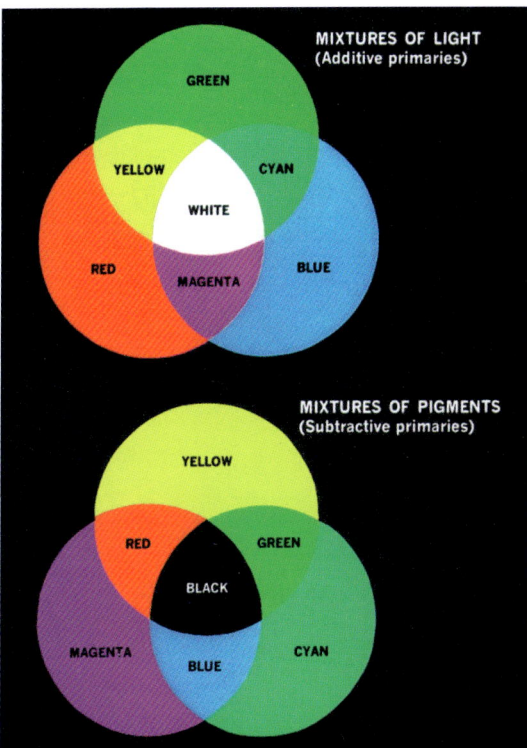

Figure 3-1: **Mixtures of Light** – additive and subtractive primaries. The primary colors of light (red, green and blue) can be added to produce the secondary colors of light: magenta (red plus blue), cyan (green plus blue) and yellow (red plus green). Thus the colors of light are called "additives." A secondary color light, mixed in the right proportions with its opposite primary, will produce white light. For example, a mixture of yellows and blue light will result in white light. Thus, yellow and blue are complementary colors of light, as are cyan and red and magenta and green. Color television reception is an example of the "additive" nature of light colors.

This subtractive nature of pigments is easily demonstrated by placing magenta, cyan and yellow pigment filters over a source of white light, as shown here. Each of the pigment filters absorbs or subtracts one of the primary colors from the light. Where two filters overlap, one of the primaries of light is transmitted. For example, a yellow filter absorbs blue (transmitting red and blue). Together, the filters transmit only red, having, in effect, subtracted the other two primary colors from the white light. Where the three pigment filters are superimposed at the center, all light is absorbed. Complementary pigment colors are the same as those in light: yellow and blue, cyan and red, magenta and green (IESNA *Lighting Handbook*, 9th Edition, 2000).

Figure 3-2:
Chihuly Lounge at
The Ritz-Carlton,
Millennia Singapore 2006

Hospitality: We see by a contrast of tone and color. The lighting designer is like a musical composer in the creating of his lighting plan. When dimming control is added, he also becomes the conductor.

REPRINTED WITH PERMISSION
OF THE RITZ-CARLTON
HOTEL COMPANY, L.L.C.

Oliver Sacks, Neurologist and Writer

"I am addicted to walking around New York at night, looking at its lights through the pocket spectroscope I carry with me everywhere. Like any prism, it splits light into its constituent colors, and I can instantly identify and relish the different spectra that result from the city's various lights. There are the beautiful sodium lamps under the bridges in Central Park that reveal, through the spectroscope, a single brilliant white line. There are the dozens of different fluorescent lights in Times Square, the great mercury vapor street lamps on the major avenues and the old-fashioned gas mantles, with their greenish yellow light, which one can find in Gramercy Park or St. Luke's Place or parts of Brooklyn. I was ambling around Greenwich Village recently, admiring the scarlet neon restaurant signs with my spectroscope (the seemingly simple light of neon reveals itself as amazingly complex, consisting of a dozen or more brilliant red and yellow lines), and I found myself the subject of puzzled attention from the patrons inside one bar.
I walked inside to explain what I was doing, and a few minutes later everyone was looking through my little spectroscope at the neon sign, at the street lamps outside and at a candle flame burning on a sidewalk table in the night."

–The New York Times, November 11, 2001

Light's most important properties

Light can be characterized by four important properties: intensity, color, distribution and movement. In his *Lighting for Architects* (1957), taught when he was a professor of lighting at Yale University, Stanley McCandless describes these four properties in terms of how light affects the operation of the eye "because by grasping the characteristics of the seeing process one can determine which elements of lighting will create the mental image desired, especially with regard to the creation and control of the range of variations the eye is able to distinguish." His design philosophy centered around these four main elements whether regarding the function, qualities, characteristics or technology of light.

Intensity is the amount of stimulation the eye can distinguish. Due to pupil and retinal accommodation, the eye can distinguish a great range of intensity from starlight illumination to brilliant sunlight, which is of the order of 1 to 1,000,000 units. An adequate scale for man-made light would be 1 to 500 units, from 0.1 to 50 footcandles.

Color is the quality of stimulation. The eye can distinguish hues, tints and shades through a long development under the subtleties of daylighting. The eye accepts a composite mixture of light rays, often the result of two or three pure colors superimposed on a surface. The palette of the lighting designer can be as simple as that of the painter as long as he is able to control the intensities and the additive mixture of each of the three primary colors: red, green and blue.

Distribution is the extent, or size and shape of stimulation. The eye reacts similarly to the sensitized film of a camera with regard to form. Retinal nerve fibers are individually sensitive to intensity and color. Two-dimensional patterns projected on the lens are affected by external conditions such as lines of perspective, position of shade and shadow, sharpness of outline, relative color and relative movement that indicate space relationships, or a three-dimensional form.

Movement is the duration or change of stimulation. This quality involves an analysis of change in intensity, color or duration. The eye needs a certain amount of time to analyze a given set of conditions, and it will always seek out the most brilliantly illuminated object in the field of vision first, because that will invariably be the most readable. Excesses in contrast and in movement tend to cause fatigue so there is a limit beyond which the helpful aspects of these qualities can be applied.

Figure 3-3: **A spectroscope with accompanying spectral power distribution, a banknote and a light meter—tools that enable you to "know light."**

4

Learning to See

A man opens his eyes, light enters and falls on the retina… the process of seeing begins.
 —paraphrased from Oliver Sacks' *An Anthropologist on Mars*, Pg. 115, C. 1995 Viking Press

SO IT IS WE SEE. Yet my experience in teaching at several universities these past 40+ years has proven to me that most of the students who came to learn lighting had never first learned to see. Oh yes, their eyesight was normal, but they were not able to demonstrate to me that they had seen much that pertained to light or lighting in their entire lives. It seemed that they had no powers of observation—myopia, it seems, not restricted to eyesight. The students, in fact, were all suffering from a form of congenital achromatopsia, a total lack of any sense of color. They all lived in a leaden cast, formless world. Since they all possessed normal eyesight, I concluded it must be a form of hysteria caused by their arrival in my class! That turned out to be untrue. It was simply that no one had taught them "to see."

There has been a trend in music this last decade for musicians to perform "unplugged"—meaning without reinforcement. The intention is to give center stage back to the human voice, so often masked by technology. To perform unplugged, a vocalist or musical group engages their audience on a more human level. It's a much more intimate and revealing forum than a typical concert. To accept the responsibility of exposing oneself in that manner requires a desire to communicate from the heart, as well as mastery of technique. All elements of the performance must strive for perfection—the voices, the lyrics, the instruments. A skilled musician can take the feeling from a lyric or a song and touch an emotional chord in some piece of each member of his audience.

Drawing, writing and making music are the food of our creative spirit. They are what inspire us to strip ourselves of rules and equipment, utilize our ability and skill to move others by our creations, inject humanity into our work. They allow us, as artists, designers, to engage everyone—including the client, our friends and family—on a more personal level, without the crutches of complex calculations or codes or standards. They can infuse us with curiosity, and cajole us into performing lighting—unplugged. In order to perform so purely, the musician must have learned to listen just as we must learn to see.

To see, you must engage your brain—an exercise that takes great discipline. Most people are blissfully unaware that they do not know how to see. So, here we shall embark on the path of learning to see, to use our powers of sight for careful observation—observation that we can summon up when required—to reorder our minds, and to restore some of the images and emotions of our past experiences for immediate recall for use in life, as in design. We must develop a sense memory.

Learn not to throw away your mind. Learn how important it is to remember places and situations. Do not discard ideas, scenes or experiences. Rather, note them in some fashion, such as notes or sketches, before you forget them. Ideas and concepts are precious. When we throw them away, by not recording them, we trash a piece of our mind. By grasping the quotidian experience you will be able to create it, enhance it and occasionally transcend it. Seek to discover the rare to be able to recreate it.

Figure 4-1.
Churches: Christ Church, Bronxville, NY.

COURTESY OF RAMBUSCH LIGHTING, FABRICATOR; BROOKE CARTER, LIGHTING DESIGNER.

Figure 4-2. **Schools: Maria de Hostos Community College, New York City.**

© PAUL WARCHOL (2)

LEARNING TO SEE: A Matter of Light

This practice of going through a methodical thought process is critical, for if you don't know how "to see," how will you determine what it is you wish to see when you try to design any system for life? The difference between good work and extraordinary work is the quality of thought and the number of hours that are brought to bear in sifting through potential design solutions—determining your vision! And then learning how to communicate that vision so that someone else can see it as well as you can.

Constantly putting yourself in the mind of a teacher who is teaching people how to see will help you learn how to see, and knowing how to see will not only shape your world, but how you present yourself to the world, and how you present "your world" to others.

Light is an element of environmental design. Color and revelation of form are the two most important elements used to integrate people in an environmental design with light. Soft glow, highlight and shadow create selective visibility, dimension, composition and mood.

Like night..
...and day.
Petronas Towers, Kuala Lumpur.

Figure 4-3. Good lighting must have elements of surprise, comfort and warmth or whatever mood the space being created must achieve.

© JEFF GOLDBER/ESTO (2). ALL RIGHTS RESERVED.

Taking Responsibility

5
Curiosity and Skepticism

"People who live their lives without being curious means they've made up their minds about everything."
—Stanley Mason, American inventor

FOR ALL THE ASSETS WE POSSESS, the greatest is our imagination, which dwells beyond technique. The challenge is to work with a mind that is open but not empty, well furnished but not set in its ways. We must think, debate issues, visit museums, follow politics, go to the theater, listen to music, travel—and above all, read, not just about our profession, but poetry, philosophy, fiction. The more we know of the world outside our discipline—about life—the better we'll be at our art. Exceptional designers are highly motivated, ambitious, curious risk-takers who have the capacity to endure the consequences of independent thinking.

We must be careful not to be so reliant on the tools of our education—the codes and standards that become so intimidating—that we no longer rely on our subjective judgment. If you accept the "Flesch Injunction," described in the Introduction, you have the instant elimination of all lighting standards. Following standards becomes a process of design that uses the thought-free methodology of just filling a prescription. Standards are what "have always been done." They neutralize creativity and personal perception. Instead, we should rely on our emotions, personal evaluations and the responses of our client. Your client, friends, associates and you have a duty to enlighten, learn from and educate each other. Show them the solutions you propose are going to make their lives better, and add beauty. Inject the human element.

Hashem Aghajari was a teacher sentenced to death in Iran for blasphemy at the beginning of the new millennium. His offense was telling his students, "In all matters… your reason is a better tool of discernment than all the sayings of prophets and clerics." He was condemned for advocating individual thought as opposed to blindly accepting the thinking—or non-thinking—of others.

Renee Descartes once said, "I think, therefore I am." Another way of looking at this is to say when we don't think, we are nothing (unfortunately, we don't disappear).

What makes great design projects candidates for immortality is that their creators went about their task with curiosity and open-mindedness. They coupled a complete lack of pretense with a nice healthy skepticism, a responsibility that should not be considered a burden, but an adventure—a chance to change the world. That should be the hallmark of your life and work.

Treat each day as though it were your first. Treat each day as though it were your last. Take architecture as an example: Think of the building you'd wish to be remembered by. The British architect, Ron Herron, said, "When you are looking for a solution to what you are told is an architectural problem, remember—it may not be a building."

To which I would add: It may be light.

Of itself, light is one of the most powerful tools in the architect's repertoire, "a new 20th-century material to be folded into the mix of architectural elements. Understood from a fundamental level, its judicious use may transcend the simple upping of visibility and satisfaction of a set of minimum conditions, and move on to orchestrate compositions and form through illusive movement of the static, enhancement through color and the overall creation and manipulation of composition, atmosphere and mood"

Figure 5-1: **404 Washington.** Using color to reinforce the space; color and color changing just for the sake of being able to do it has no real purpose other than glitz. It is far better to use the light as reinforcer of a space than to use the space as the backdrop for the light.

PHOTOGRAPHY COURTESY OF WWW.SCOTTBSMITHPHOTO.COM (2)

(K. Simonson, 1997). Light can flatter, soothe, stimulate, conceal or reveal. It can ensure safety on the factory floor and can create an island of calm in a hectic office. Lighting can alter our perception of place, comfort and security.

When you, as "designer," undertake a new project—your own home, for example—lighting solutions must be a part of your thinking from the start. Remember that you are training yourself "to see." Learn to see well to better understand and perhaps to serve well. Learn to light well by being alert to what works and doesn't work, wherever you go.

Keep your eyes—and your mind—open and evaluate every visual experience. When something looks right, ask yourself: What kind of light is that? Where is it coming from? What is its source, location, distribution, direction, intensity? How does it make people look? How does it act upon materials and color?

Absorb what you have seen, then translate it into personal terms, remembering that no single solution fits all scenarios. The play of light on a travertine wall will be different from that same light shining on grass cloth, and what is right for a romantic French restaurant would be disastrous in a fast food restaurant. Ultimately, you must work your way through to the solution that is particular to you.

So study. Analyze. Reflect. Edit and invent. The works of others can serve as a guide, a catalyst or an inspiration, but you are obliged to go forth and create something new. I quote from Alice's Red Duchess: "It's a poor sort of memory that only works backwards." Remember, the only worthwhile solutions are the ones you arrive at yourself.

This solo journey can be difficult, but rewarding as well.

Joze Plecnik, the distinguished Vienna secessionist architect, noted, "I have always observed, whenever I had the opportunity, how the work of great people—not only architects, but also of painters—starts with unclarity, how suffering ensues and how, later, after some concentration, man liberates himself into such a simple form that one would never have thought that it had required some effort."

What is required here is some "suffering." Who wants to create what has already been seen before? Who wants their work to be recognized as a copy?

Awaken the desire within you to be special. To do that, you need to be curious and to carry a heightened sense of skepticism. If all you wish to do is to parrot what your friends, teachers or earlier researchers have done, you have no worries; you won't suffer, but you won't excel either.

6
The Horse's Mouth

"I Found a Million-Dollar Baby in a 5 and 10 Cent Store."
—Title of a song by Harry Warren

WHEN I NEED TO KNOW SOMETHING about lighting, I never consult a lighting person. Regardless of the subject, I go to the stable and seek out a wise person—an artist, philosopher, poet or scientist who has made a great contribution in his or her field. I would rather know what Goethe, Steinmetz or Einstein thought about lighting than one of my peers. That is how I expand my perspective on the application of light.

If I need technical information, I seek out the most renowned source alive—the person who generated what it is I need to know—the horse itself, so to speak. Seeking that wisdom has become my method of learning to see better and assuaging that curiosity that enriches all design.

Research is vital to the authenticity and credibility of your work. Enlightenment, therefore, should come by way of authentic sources; especially valuable is the help you'll get from a good librarian at a first-class library. Each new term, I have my students take part in the "Horse's Mouth Lottery," an exercise devised by Diane Lewis, Professor of Architecture at Cooper Union College in New York City, and refined by me. Students would draw names out of a hat: DaVinci, Einstein, Homer, Hume, Freud and Stanislavski, to name a few. Their assignment is to find some "quotable quotes" by that person that serve as metaphors, analogies or allegorical references to the subject of the art, science and practice of light and lighting, then describe their significance. In life, in pursuit of knowledge, why not go straight to the horse's mouth?

Do you even know who the horses are? There's generally more than one horse, and they make the best mentors. Otherwise, you might be getting information from the other end of the horse.

Who will be your mentor? In any profession in life, we have choices and challenges. Who are the heroes of what you do?

Choose someone you admire. Look to the gods in your field. In the Golden Age of Painting, young artists apprenticed themselves to masters. Thus Raphael apprenticed to Perugina, Michelangelo to Ghirlandaiao. They chose their mentors wisely, then out-performed them. This is as it should be.

> Incorrigible curiosity goes a long way. What is there to lose? Whenever I select a book to read, I buy at least two copies—one to annotate and one to keep pristine. And when I annotate, there is little white space left on a page, with questions, comments and impressions scribbled and squeezed into whatever the margins will allow. And it doesn't stop there; I often contact the author to share my questions and comment on the off chance that they may reply. And they often do. This has led to wonderful and unexpected encounters in the most random of places—a stimulating dinner meeting in New York City, a rendezvous at an airport in Europe—with some of the most brilliant minds that exist today, luminaries whose names have been peppered throughout this rather long essay. The horse's mouth may only be an e-mail away.

Some of my earliest mentors were my high school teachers. My art teacher, Leon Freund, taught me to see. He would say, "In front of you is a blank piece of paper, an opportunity to create a work of art. Let's see what you can do." I was taught that the artist must have some kind of order, or he or she will create a very ordinary body of work. Creating art requires labor—hard labor, labor based on discipline and order.

Lighting design is an art.

Designed architectural lighting systems began to flourish in the early 20th-century. Names like Stanley McCandless, Richard Kelly, Bill Richardson, John Waldrum—to name a few—were designing lighting systems that were poetry to behold. There were only a few. I was fortunate enough to have known most of them as mentors while retaining those I "befriended" in college while studying philosophy—great minds like Plato and Pythagoras.

The master's job is to raise the bar; the student's job is to surpass. No matter how young or old you are, don't be afraid to go after the giants in your field, or into disciplines other than your own—art, philosophy, physics—if there's something to be learned. Don't hesitate to step outside your field in the pursuit of knowledge, expanding your appreciation of your universe.

It's important to note, however, that even the most open-minded mentor will have a particular point of view to promote. Remember, the only solutions worth having are the ones you arrive at independently. We can't replicate the glories of another era but we can be informed by the same notions of excellence.

The words of Matsuo Basho, samurai and master Haiku poet, come to mind: "Do not seek to follow in the footsteps of the old; seek what they sought." We can understand, interpret, create—but not copy.

Getting Creative

7
Conjuring Up the Image

"There will always be new dogmas cropping up in lighting. Fortunately, not everyone will become disciples."
—the author

WE ARE SPATIAL CREATURES. We navigate spaces daily and assess them, resonating with those in which we feel most comfortable. Whether conscious of it or not, in designing our own lives we have developed an understanding of relationships between space and people's responses to space. It is the application of that understanding that initiates the design process.

The design process can be distilled into two major phases: creation and implementation. As part of "creation," you must naturally conjure up an image of what it is you wish to see. Before even approaching the project, you must clear your mind completely of any ideas that will prejudice the creation of an extraordinary, unique design solution—the birthright of every design. It is too tempting to allow the remnants of memory to prejudice your thinking. Having any preconceived notion at all of how to configure the space or place furnishings or light objects will lead to failure. The words "doctor's office" right now may automatically recall another doctor's office in your mind, the location of the reception desk, the color of the upholstery on the chairs and how the waiting room was lighted. Wrong! That's sabotage of the highest order. Control the synaptic response; don't let it intrude on the freshness of a new thought process.

"I think, therefore I am." Within those thoughts, imagination must be a component. Where did this "imagination" come from? What, in life's experiences, conjured up a particular imaginative notion at that particular moment? And what in the formative years of our upbringing put up boundaries to surround that moment and make it a place in our lives? While we must rely on our imagination to conjure up memories from that mental database we are continually building, to convey what we wish to see, we must also practice discipline at the onset of each new project. Draw on the database of memory, yet refrain from applying the fruits of those memories prematurely. While sounding contradictory, it is a crucial part of the process. For if we look at something, yet can't see it, we have no point of reference, no level of understanding. Imagine Native Americans of 1492 seeing a European ship for the first time—they would have no comprehension of it, no memory reflex, therefore how could they really "see" it?

Do we spontaneously blurt out or otherwise take immediate action to any stimulus, or do we, by that early training, place the ring of inhibition around ourselves to temper what we will do? Frank Lloyd Wright warned of the "floo-floo" bird, the peculiar and special bird which always flew backward "because it didn't give a darn where it was going, but just had to see where it had been." Isn't that precisely how we often do our work? We look at what has been done and under what rules, where we have always been, instead of ahead to the purpose of our original intentions.

Make it a practice to clear your mind repeatedly. It is a real mental exercise, just like learning to see. We should be constantly training our brains.

8

Subconscious to Conscious

"Beauty is a better introduction than any letter of recommendation." —Aristotle

WE ARE DISTINGUISHED BY OUR DIFFERENCES. There is a story concerning Albert Einstein and the great concert pianist Artur Schnabel. Einstein was an enthusiastic violinist and, on this particular occasion, he invited Schnabel to come play duets with him. So Schnabel went to Princeton. He sat down at the piano. Einstein got out his fiddle. I have no doubt there was a keen sense of anticipation in that room as the two giants of their day set about tackling some Beethoven. But they had only been playing a few minutes when Schnabel slammed down the lid of the keyboard and turned around to Einstein in disgust. "What's the matter with you, Albert?" he barked. "Can't you count? Ah—one…two…three…four…"

Clearly, there is *counting* and then there is counting—each artist to his own method. Think of Dante, Shakespeare, Wordsworth and Keats. Within the literary form recognized as poetry, they tested the confines to produce creative brilliance from sonnet to iambic pentameter.

Lighting design will be used as an example in this chapter. To do so, we must first define good lighting. The single most significant problem in the design of any lighting system today generally lies in an understanding of the definition of good lighting. Simply put, the lighting should be of benefit to the project—a part of the design for people and spaces. We live in a visual culture; lighting plays a major role in seeing.

Good lighting is defined at the beginning of each project with each user. It then has a chance to become exemplary lighting.

The design process is a disciplined execution of what you do. To even begin to have a successful project, the users and design team must collaborate, identify issues, share ideas and establish a common language. The users could show the design team at least three examples of places they like. Then the design team could show them three or four alternate places until everyone reaches an understanding of space light levels, expectations. This exercise may reveal surprising disparities in perception learning what it is you wish to see.

> If everything is a construct of the mind, the problem is we're not observant enough to create an inventory of materials to construct properly; everybody's brain has an infinite capacity, there's just a glitch in our access memory.

This interaction will let you identify the unique characteristics that distinguish the user's requirements from other people's opinions. It is simply a sifting through of ideas and examples that enables all parties involved to narrow the decisions to just the one solution they plan to install. All parties must have a presence in order to "sift" thoroughly.

The lighting design process will be unique to the individual being served, producing a unique result. Since all people are not alike, neither are their work tasks, leisure pursuits or the places they like. Hence, there is no single solution that will solve all lighting problems, and there is certainly no prescribed answer. Although numbers may theoretically describe the complexity of the human visual system, they cannot cope with personal perception. When trying to find a visual solution that is deeply satisfying in human terms, "numbers methodology" is suspect. That is why we must use a practice methodology containing an interactive component that includes the user and all members of the design team to enable testing of all potential design solutions.

The ultimate test, therefore, is: Did the lighting design satisfy each of your needs or the user's particular needs and wants for his project? Was every decision or choice correct for the application? Was a reasonable method developed to test the above questions? If so, the resultant lighting was probably good. While there are no rules for good lighting, there are some criteria that can be used as guidelines and help elevate it from ordinary to extraordinary.

9
Space: Substructure of a Greater Whole

"Light has an almost miraculous flexibility. It possesses all degrees of clarity, all possibilities of color, all the variations of a palette. It can produce shadows and distribute the harmony of its vibrations in space as music does."
—Adolph Appia

SPACE IS SOMETHING THAT ALWAYS surrounds you. It is the volume in which you exist at the moment you are there. It is an alleyway, narrow and high. It is a corridor, wide and low. It is a museum, tunnel, temple, closet. It is mobile as well as stationary, like walking up a narrow street in Hong Kong; it is hilly, tactile. It is going up a grand flight of stairs at the opera and under the balcony. It is entering the clearing in the woods. It is exploring the cave in the mountain. It is leaving the lobby and getting into an elevator. It is walking into your office. It is visiting your boss's office.

Any space you design, whether personally or professionally, must be considered holistically, the synergy between inextricable elements. There will be an interaction between zones, from exterior to interior, from cafeteria to auditorium, from the basement to the second floor. What happens at each stage of motion? Analyze the area and its adjacencies thoroughly. Begin with step one:

How will the people first see the place in question and what is the first impression to be? How do you get there? Walk? Take the train, then a taxi? What do you do once you arrive? Go down the stairs, up the escalator, wait in the lobby, get in an elevator? Is it a glass elevator? Consider each step of the route: How will the space be entered and what should people experience at this critical point? Where will people proceed to and how can their passage be made efficient, comfortable, stimulating or perhaps tranquil? Then consider the transition from one zone to another: Does the function of each change drastically? How are the spaces affected by time of day: Are they windowed, shielded by shades and drapes? Are the walls dark, carpets light? Is there a lot of mingling activity or are most occupants busy working on computers in their cubicles?

This is just a sampling of questions that should guide you as you assess the issues, regardless of whether you are designing an interior, the architecture, the lighting or "just" life's spaces. Subliminally or consciously, we are always assessing.

Once you determine what is happening inside and outside the boundaries of a space, you might ask: How will the lighting affect it? How will the various spaces be used and what mood should each convey? Does the lighting reinforce the architecture? Does it aid the productivity of the worker? Will the interior building lighting affect the streets immediately surrounding it? Will the exterior building lighting compete with the street lighting? Will it benefit or hurt the adjacent retail stores? Will it project beyond the immediate neighborhood? How will pedestrians strolling out from a nearby theater view the scene? Such analysis applies to any project you attempt, from your own house to the places you shop and dine, from a high-rise office building or a single-story dwelling to a shopping mall, monument or city park.

Light is an element that unifies and differentiates space, creates a focus, develops a hierarchy and has movement. Its patterns have rhythm: steady and repetitive or quick and staccato. Light can create or dissipate ephemeral boundaries, it can define the difference between inside and outside

("Interior space is presented either as a continuum of exterior space, or contrasted with it," wrote Marietta S. Millet in *Light Revealing Architecture*, 1996). Early in the 20th century, Frank Lloyd Wright and members of the Prairie School used a lot more large windows than customary at the time to connect the inside and outside with distinctly framed views. People need a connection to the outdoors—biophilia. Design is all about human beings.

Walk the route of the people using a space to learn how actions determine needs. Each person views the same space differently: A customer in a store has a different agenda than a salesperson. As an example, pretend there is a furniture store that hires you as lighting designer in hopes of increasing its sales by improving its lighting. Playing the role of customer allows you to understand what it means to be a customer, gather information such as the routes taken through the store, impressions of the spaces and the sales methodology encountered. This experience becomes the foundation for designing an effective, in this case "productive," lighting scheme, as Kit Kuttle and I discovered while studying lighting's impact on productivity in a retail environment in 1995 (resulting in a technical paper that earned the Illuminating Engineering Society of North America's Taylor Technical Talent Award).

Upon entry into the store, the customer is greeted by a salesperson. That salesperson is the customer's guide through the store. The store is laid out in a series of galleries, with groupings of kitchen, dining, living room and bedroom furniture in each gallery. Rather than the furniture being the main attraction, what a customer sees while on this tour is a clutter of hanging light fixtures and the glare of exposed lamps from endless lines of track, and only an obscured view of some furniture. People find that they can neither clearly see the space they are in nor the people they are with. To select fabrics, customers must either go outside or to a window.

Navigating the store, it becomes obvious that the furniture displays and prices change, yet the lighting doesn't; all the spaces and merchandise are lighted identically. There are no contrasts or accents on special merchandise. Our challenge is to modify each area by its lighting to produce visual clarity and a changing, dynamic itinerary throughout the store in order to induce sales. Our primary imperative is to create galleries that are so comfortable to shop in that they become the destination of choice for all the sales personnel. We can subtly and deliberately alter the traffic patterns of customers through lighting. So, by reducing the visual clutter and providing a dynamic, energy-conscious lighting design, the sales staff finds those areas very pleasant and they now take their customers there. People discern colors in fabrics better and no longer have to go outside or to windows to verify their choices. Bottom line is: The store sells more merchandise as a direct result of the increase in traffic—a little enlightenment, flavored with sales.

Before each project, clear your mind. Then decide what it is you wish to see as both a user and worker in the space.

10
A Sense of Place

"Give me a place to stand on, and I will move the earth."
—Archimedes

WE MUST DEFINE "OFFICE" so that we can design it. So what is an office? Is it where your computer and files reside? Think more broadly: The greater meaning of office is not necessarily a place. An office in the public sector is a position or place that symbolizes a duty, trust or function. It is a combination of people and location that provides the service or business of public sector endeavor. Consider first the Army, the Department of State, the Department of Justice and then the Department of Agriculture. Each conjures up a different image (symbol) and functional responsibility. This image and duty is inherent in that "office." Each part of the public sector has its own unique qualities which must be respected and reinforced in its workplace. Each unique individual who works there has a calling, a desire to serve and an obligation to uphold his or her "office" and sustain it. Here there is an investment of emotion in creating a persona, a commitment to justice and a sense of pride. To ensure that this symbol of "office" and officeholder is realized, a system must be created that can deal with each location as an entity from conception to occupancy, management and maintenance. Each location or group of locations, as in a large facility, must be created and remain under the direction of the people it was built to serve, including their successors. This single step will personalize the "office" and reinforce its status of position and appropriateness of structure. The physical office space's usefulness and habitability are measured by how well it serves the people and "office." Standards, maximizing energy savings or designing to any number of other fashionable systems are useless. A good office is created in the spirit of the service—an appropriate place to do what needs to be done.

"Office" is special; it is a person occupying a space, such as the attorney general or head of urban development. That person needs a location to dispense his or her services and that location is different from one person to the next because their professional cultures are different, uniquely special. The office is the public sector's largest product—service.

How do you go about designing such a place? You do so systematically and in categorical order. Describe the big picture. Envision a region, such as a county in your state. Within this region, there is most likely a city, farther out are the suburbs and beyond those are rural areas. Where does this "office" fall within this structure? If it is located in the city, it will have a certain style; if in the suburbs, another.

Figure 10-1. Understanding "office" requires an understanding of its extended environment. One way to achieve this is to document the commute of typical workers to the office you're designing—what do they see? What do they do? What is being offered to them?   PHOTOGRAPHS COURTESY OF P. RIZZO (6)

Figure 10-2.
Government offices:
Rendering of Courthouse
in Syracuse, New York.

Next step: Is it a private or public office? Under public offices, we can list institutions, such as government and education. Under private, we have corporations and other business entities. Each will display individual characteristics. They should neither function identically nor be inhabited or furnished identically.

In order to design anything well, to create uniquely with purpose and intent, this all-inclusive method of thinking is required.

Museums

Harmony has often been equated with beauty. In music, sculpture, painting and in nature itself, the end result has usually been identified as harmony. The ingredients of flow—of rhythm, balance, of symmetry (and asymmetry) and perspective—tend to contribute to a harmonious whole. Creative lighting can learn a great deal from nature and from the arts in achieving its own intrinsic harmony and beauty.

A museum, as an example, is the chronicle and exhibition of man and his world. A walk through a maze of uniformly lighted, monotonous corridors will induce museum fatigue in even the most enthusiastic art lover. As a fine symphony must carefully be conceived and executed, so must the design of a museum be composed with great sensitivity to the physical environment which houses the art. This design must be concerned not only with the preservation of the work exhibited, but with the people viewing it and the harmonious blend of space, light and objects as well. It is with light that art is perceived, and a contrast of lighting qualities, quantities and focuses can make a space stimulating or fatiguing. Equally important is the diversity of spaces: The shape and size of a room, and how it relates to the series of rooms adjoining it, can make a visitor hurry through or calmly view an exhibit. What one is looking for is a stimulating experience.

It's ironic how the distant past continues to enlighten our present and future.

"The hottest hit show in New York these days isn't *Rent* or The *Lion King* or indeed anything on Broadway—but remains the magnificently restored and re-lighted Fossil Halls at the American Museum of Natural History. Opened to celebrate the Museum's 125th Anniversary, the exhibit plays to packed houses—week in and week out—and Tyrannosaurus Rex is unquestionably the biggest star in town."

Figure 10-3 **Fossil Hall, American Museum of Natural History, New York City.**
© SCOTT FRANCES/ESTO ALL RIGHTS RESERVED.

These introductory words belied the title of H.M. Brandston & Partners' 1999 report, "Lighting and Shade Control Energy Conservation Study," at the American Museum of Natural History. The study, conducted from 1992 to 1999, encompassed Fossil Halls 5, 9 and 13 of the Museum. A project whose objective was energy conservation resulted in so much more by approaching the issues holistically—and from the core, not the perimeter—by finding the balance between technology and the spirit of the space. It resulted from being able to "see" what needed to be done and by doing what made sense.

Our approach was to focus lighting attention not on what was being exhibited but by who was going to view it—by making it exciting for them! Inspiration sprouted from a vision of all the children who are bussed there everyday, the image of them running through the bones like electric mice, zooming through the halls. That was our goal, in combination with attempting to respect architect Pope's original lighting design, which meant keeping light levels low, and yes, using all incandescent. Seems to defy current definitions of energy conservation, doesn't it? Wait and see.

Imagine a 1950s renovation in which windows were bricked up, acoustic tiles obliterated decorative ceilings and fluorescent fixtures took the place of elegant chandeliers and period sconces—basically, an aesthetic fiasco. Still, the Fossil Halls remained a magnet for millions of school children, museum buffs, scholars and out-of-town visitors. New York City's Jurassic Park was always a prime attraction, but the unfortunate surroundings failed to do the great collection justice. Our approach in this latest restoration was to convey a sense of "you are there" to every museum-goer—to recreate a space and atmosphere in which one could truly envision what it was like when prehistoric creatures stalked the earth and all else trembled. And though humans and dinosaurs never co-existed in real life, in a sense they did now in the halls of the American Museum of Natural History.

We hoped to achieve this illusion by combining the best attributes of old and new to restore the soaring architectural grandeur of the 19th-century halls, while enhancing the museum-goers' experience by employing the most recent advancements in lighting and control technology, both daylight and electric. Our objective was to create a display that would combine learning and beauty and environmental sensitivity with a touch of showmanship. Simply put, our principal goal was to create spaces that people would love and wish to return to. This is the very essence of productivity. It also clearly illustrates good energy optimization design methodology. So it could be stated, somewhat euphemistically, that these prehistoric fossils ultimately contributed to the improvement of our air quality and the present environment as we approached the 21st century.

The result was both a critical and popular success unique in any museum's history. The technical results of the energy demonstration research were worthy of similar acclaim.

Creative use of lighting was among the primary elements that made the Fossil Halls such a resounding triumph. Here we had used a combination of the past and mixed in a little of the present. Fortunately, some of the original chandeliers were discovered stored in the museum's basement, so their replacements could be constructed with a sense of the museum's history but not reproductions of the originals. The windows were unbricked and the original fenestration restored, thus allowing daylight into the halls and reducing daytime lighting needs. And daylight, of course, added to the verisimilitude of the "you are there" experience. With modified replicas of chandeliers and sconces back in place, with the newly opened windows as a source of daylight, all that was required by way of 20th-century fixtures was the addition of a few accentlights, along with daylight and electric light intensity control devices.

To see sunlight streaming through the ancient bones was to make the past come alive in a richly emotional way. And the automated light and shade control system allowed not only the sun and sky to provide most of the lighting, but to set electric lighting intensities to best create a mood for the visitors' viewing of all the different exhibits. We were thus able to use far less than Illuminating Engineering Society-recommended light levels. This is a significant fact to note in terms of the value in dollars and reduction of use of energy. It is also critical to be aware that we were able to reduce the late night light levels as well as those during daylight hours.

As a result of the lighting control system mediating the available light with electric lighting, light levels between five and 20 footcandles were, on average, maintained in each hall throughout the open hours of the museum. Consequently, both energy consumption and cost were reduced, on average, approximately 50 percent in each of the three halls. That translated to more than $14,000 in annual energy cost savings. Not bad for revitalizing old bones—and just doing what made sense.

City...planning urban lighting

A city is defined by the people whose feet traverse the pavement and observe the surrounds they pass through. Those definitions can vary from metropolis to urban sprawl to asphalt jungle. I grew up in New York in the 1940s. New York was a vibrant, open, inviting, cultural resource. It was a welcome, unthreatening, safe place to partake of all that she had to offer. How lucky I was. Times have changed, and now is the time to see what contribution lighting can make to enhance the quality of life in our cities.

One of the services a city provides for its residents and visitors is to light its streets. It does this to provide illumination for passage and security. During the day, these lampposts become a part of the furniture of the street. At night, they almost vanish in the contrast of the bright discharge of the light source. The street scene, more often than not, unfolds as a sequence of starkly shadowed gloom. It should be otherwise.

Louis Mumford said: "A city exists, not for the passage of motorcars, but for the care and culture of man." And he was right. A city is the living room and cultural resource for the region it is centered within. Its streets are the playpen for the children of its residents. For that is where their children grow up, and day by day learn the social interaction and responsibility that will make them productive members of society. When you choose your city's lighting system, you have made one of the most significant decisions for the well-being of its street life, because that lighting is an all-pervasive part of what you will see, both in the daytime and at night. When you make those design decisions, you will have furnished and lighted the living room of your city and its outskirts.

The primary purpose of urban lighting is to create illuminated scenes that provide a safer, more inviting, attractive, appropriate and positive image for the people who live and work in the neighborhoods that the light serves. How do you choose what you wish to light and the light itself, and how do you compose a city with it? It takes more than just light to see. You must first learn to make subjective value judgments based on what you see—judgments about the appearance of people, objects and the places being lighted and the variety of equipment that is providing the light.

Consider, for a moment the wisdom of Dr. Seuss:

> *Now that you are here, the word of the Lorax*
>   *seems perfectly clear:*
> *Unless someone like you cares a whole awful lot,*
> *Nothing is going to get better.*
> *It's not.*

My goal as lighting designer is not just to design a good lighting system, but to bring something to the project at hand that was unanticipated by the recipients of my lighting design services. What real benefit is one to the design team or the client for any project if all one does it provide them with lighting information? Average benefit only! After all, one is only doing exactly what is expected.

Try to bring that "unanticipated contribution" to your work that the client or design team was not looking to come from you. Demonstrate that you truly wish to be considered a member of the team. Let them know that you will do whatever you can to assist them in their enterprise. Simply put, try to be a person who is good to have around no matter what the situation. Notice I did not say anything about lighting design.

In 1993, *The New York Times* reported on a relighted section of Manhattan for which I did the lighting: "Conventional wisdom says nobody is getting higher rents for commercial space today than they did a few years ago. But don't tell that to Tom Kelly. Mr. Kelly…owns the landmarked… building at the…corner of 40th Street and Avenue of the Americas. Until a year or so ago, four of the building's floors were empty and, at asking prices of about $10 a foot, tenants were barely nibbling. Then last year, the refurbished Bryant

Park opened up across the street. ... 'I've started asking for $24...and I've got a deal going for $27, said Mr. Kelly.'" That is one of the benefits, measured in end-user economic terms, which was an anticipated result of the design plan. The prediction for change in the neighborhood helped to raise an additional $1.8 million to realize the lighting scheme.

With this philosophy in mind—that we should measure everything we do—I would like to recall the words of Daniel H. Burnham for the next principle: "Make no little plans; they have no magic to stir men's blood, and probably themselves will not be realized. Make big plans; aim in hope and work, remembering that a noble, logical diagram once recorded will never die, but long after we are gone, will be a living thing, asserting itself with ever-growing insistency. Remember that your sons and grandsons are going to do things that would stagger us. Let your watchword be order and your beacon beauty."

Upon understanding these principles, you are now ready to put your arms around your cities to design, furnish and light them. You should put forth a vision and unfold a composition that will endure, create plans that can be built upon and develop systems to measure the success of every area within this large scale adventure. From parks to commercial shopping districts, from financial zones to theater districts, from densely populated residential areas to tree-lined neighborhoods, you can begin your sketch composition. Identify the grand civic buildings for accent, ferret out the historical sites that need to be recognized—the community church and so on—until every important structure and pattern of use has been made clear by the appropriate application of light as a graphic and the selection of lighting accoutrements as street furniture. The result must be a sense of security, ease of passage and sense of location made possible by the fact that you can see clearly, and each disparate area of your city has been made recognizable by the distinctive character of its lighting.

The above sounds wonderful but is wishful thinking unless you can get it done. Lighting planning is not an exercise in democracy. I'll give you two examples of methods I've used to get projects like this built. It is the sole province and responsibility of the person/people selected to prepare the master plan guidelines to get it accepted by their client. They need to set down the principles for that acceptance at the outset of the commission with their client. A lighting master plan should not need the planner alone to prepare the design schemes. Other designers' solutions, within the plan guidelines, usually add a richness to the final result, if carefully administered. The plan must recognize the role of all the municipal agencies in the final document, but their input, if any, should in no way interfere with the proposed benefits the plan was prepared to bring about.

When we were preparing the lighting master plan for Detroit, I was asked if I wanted to consult with the departments of Parks, Transportation, Electricity, Police, ad infinitum. I responded that I most definitely did—after the preliminary plan was completed and presented to the Mayor, responsible elected officials and the residents of the city. I was immediately asked why, and replied that I did not wish to be a referee of interdepartmental turf wars over who controlled the lighting and what it should be. I just wanted to do the analysis, prepare a draft of the plan and offer it up for criticism. This was agreed upon and it worked. It worked because indeed there had been years of bureaucratically run planning that had taken place with little to show for it. The basic processes by which government agencies work tend to hamper any progress, especially those where cross-agency disciplines are required to complete a project. I was working alone and was able, as an individual, to respond to all their needs. This approach got the approval of the lighting master plan.

Another example is Bryant Park, located behind the main research branch of the New York Public Library. This is the project I mentioned earlier. The park was going to be rebuilt as it was being excavated to add stack space for the library. I was asked if I would like to do the lighting design for the park and they told me the total budget for the project was $250,000. I said of course, without a blink, even though I knew you could not begin to properly light the park, or even do the electrical distribution required, for that amount of money. The Bryant Park Business Improvement District occupies a critical central mass in the borough of Manhattan and here was an opportunity to encourage economic development that couldn't be let pass without some intervention.

I intervened: A relighting program was simultaneously planned for the park neighborhood at my suggestion. I drew a scheme that had an estimated cost of $2 million and took it to the Chairman of the Library Board to show what should be done. I explained that a design for a budget of $250,000 would be totally inadequate and inappropriate since they had just spent $60 million to bury stacks under the park; a little more fund-raising might be in order, I suggested. This was agreed to, on the spot, and we went out separately and together and raised the additional funds to do the job right. It doesn't hurt to take an active role in this aspect of lighting planning if you expect some parts of your work to be built. G.K. Chesterton said, "If the only tool you have is a hammer, you will view every problem as a nail." It takes eyesight turned into a vision to create wonderful schemes. A little light does help, but it is incidental to the dream.

11
Two points of View

"If a man will begin with certainties, he shall end in doubts; but if he will be content to begin with doubts, he shall end in certainties." —Francis Bacon

FOR STANLEY MCCANDLESS, in *Lighting for Architects* (1957), light can be considered a structural material much like brick, steel or concrete, having certain characteristics that determine its use and design. He believes the architect should design lighting as he designs the use of these materials.

According to McCandless, the functions of lighting—visibility, comfort, composition and atmosphere—define it. Light gives visibility; without light, objects cannot be seen. Bare lamps are functional, but can make us uncomfortable. Good electric lighting can actually create greater comfort than even daylight, since daylight is not as easily controlled. With lighting, the designer can create visual composition—reveal some things, suppress others—and change the appearance of otherwise static objects. He can create an appropriate atmosphere, whatever that may be. These functions are used as part of daily design whether consciously or not. In our homes, we'll place a table or floor lamp of sufficient wattage in a darkened room so that we can *see*. We'll cover it with a shade to shield the brightness from our eyes in order to make it *comfortable*. We position it in the most advantageous location in the room and choose a particular shade color so that it *looks good*. By doing so, and in concert with other elements in the room, we have created *atmosphere*. (See Appendix I for a component McCandless did not include: glare).

Visibility, comfort, composition and atmosphere are functions that give motive and critical objective to the many uses of light for the benefit of people. Techniques and equipment will constantly change and improve, "but the functions of lighting are the immutable standards of physiological, psychological and aesthetic reaction to the use of light. The approach to the mind in terms of vision is through the eye. Thus the relation of the qualities of light (the physiological aspects of seeing) to each of the properties/functions is the key to design of all uses of light," McCandless writes.

These functions extend the uses of lighting beyond that of just giving visibility. To each function is attached the four qualities of light: intensity, color, distribution and movement, clearly emphasizing that lighting is not about the equipment; it's about the light. The fixtures selected must be judged and evaluated in their context.

The personality of each lighting application is singular. While McCandless offers a method, it is not the only method. And it need not always be taken literally. Guess, estimate, measure. Have the courage to think for yourself. Say: If I could change one thing in this space, what would that be: the lighting, the furniture, the finishes? In that way, you really get to see the space from different perspectives. It is a sifting through process. Once you inject your philosophy, notions and ideas, you can mold what you've learned empirically into a wondrous new creation. No brainwashing by rules or standards, but a mélange of skill, experience and the ability to see.

In his diminutive essay, "In Praise of Shadows," published in 1933, Japanese novelist Jun'ichiro Tanizaki names darkness as an indispensable element of beauty. When dining on soup under electric light in a famous restaurant in Kyoto, a wonderful piece of black lacquerware, flecked with silver and gold, appeared to him "garish or vulgar. But render pitch black the void in which they stand, and light them not with the rays of the sun or electricity but rather a single lantern or candle: Suddenly those garish objects turn somber, refined, dignified." This phenomenon came from a deep understanding of the effect of a unique light source on the layering of blacks, browns and reds—a candle's flame. Candlelight created the desired visibility, familiar comfort, delicate composition and intimate atmosphere that electric light could not provide to this guest. The intensity: low; the distribution: uneven; the color: golden; the movement: flickering. Lighting these simple bowls of soup to any prescribed standards would have annihilated a moment of beauty and sensitivity to the aesthetics of old Japanese culture. The Japanese artisans centuries ago knew what they wished to see and how they wished to see it.

Electric light is often referred to as "artificial" light. Never have I known anything but natural light, whether daylight, firelight or man-made. All light is real, no matter how fabricated. Nowhere is it written that lighting design requires electric light or that any design requires the expected. Knowing what you wish to see—using whatever tools necessary to achieve it—imparts your open mind, background and knowledge to the experience. Customize your method to a shared vision of the moment—between you, the design team and the individuals who will enjoy the design.

Finally, know at the beginning of each project how you will measure success. You and the team should know that particular to each project. Then design for the depth of the response, not the illuminated surface. We should all remember this in the frenzy of our day to day. Close your eyes and imagine, feel and then create. Don't worry if you forget; something will trigger your sense memory. That which you are constantly, ultimately striving for is a creative solution. That only comes from confidence in your own self-judgment.

Communication

12
Designing With Light

"It is difficult to make a mark in lighting today because so many people at the top are really of bottom quality. It is time to bring out the ladders."
—the author

A GOOD LIGHTING DESIGN is realized if:

- All spaces (e.g., entry, transition, linger, work and exit) are properly composed in a clear hierarchy of importance and purpose.
- The lighting provides spatial clarity.
- The lighting mood is consistent with the function and design of each space.
- It promotes productivity.
- It is within the user's budget.
- It has fully utilized the potential of daylight when available.
- It is readily maintainable.
- It is energy effective.
- All state-of-the-art alternatives have been considered.

The Lighting Design Process can be separated into three main phases: *Advance Planning Analysis, Schematic Design*

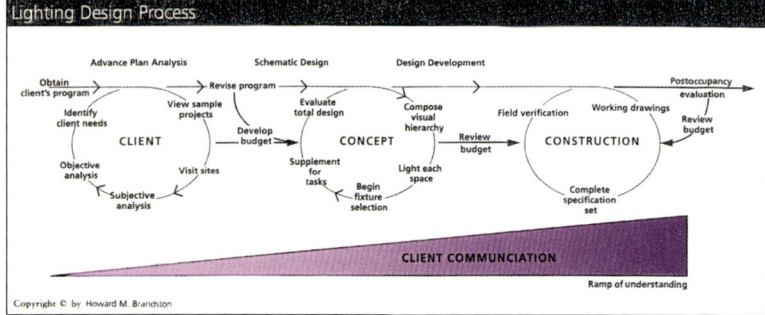

Figure 12-1. Lighting design process by Kevin Simonson and refined by the author. The interrelating "wheels" of the process are always turning, usually at different speeds.

and *Design Development*, paralleled by Client Communication, illustrated as a ramp of understanding in Figure 12-1.

Thinking ahead is crucial to a project's success. The following is a suggested list—your own or someone else's needs to be developed to suit each project.

Advance plan analysis

Focus on the relationship between the user and his or her space, which could be anything from a residence or an office to a museum, park or a zoo:

- Obtain and analyze the user's program.
- Have the user select several projects that they feel demonstrate good practice relative to his undertaking.
- Select several projects that demonstrate good practice.
- Visit the sites selected to build a vocabulary for describing lighting with likes and dislikes. Photograph locations for easy reference.
- Perform an objective analysis.
    - From selected project spaces, note building materials and measure illuminance, general surround; illuminance, local surround; task illuminance; illuminance of transition and linger areas, etc.
    - Begin selecting specifics from sites visited that relate appropriately to the client's needs, and eliminate others.

- Do a subjective analysis with staff at each location, e.g.:
  - Do you like your workspace, and why?
  - Is the lighting appropriate for space function, and why?
  - Is it comfortable to work here, and why?
  - What would you change if you could, and why? Etc.
- Do a subjective and objective analysis of the client's existing facilities.
- Establish a budget.
- Rewrite project program based on observations and measurements.

The visits and subsequent analyses described above are most important to any project.

It is an education for both designer and user, and offers the opportunity to heighten each stakeholder's awareness of lighting's role in the project about to be built. It translates the program into a set of visual experiences instead of being merely words. It will also point out to the designer the degree of difficulty that the design of the project presents—i.e., the solutions that should be considered, such as code interpretations prior to seeking variances to code restrictions that would otherwise prohibit the successful completion of the project.

> Lighting has to be appropriate for the space. There are hundreds of fixtures available in several categories: uplights, downlights, chandeliers, pendants, sconces, ceiling mount, floor lamps, table lamps, indirect, direct, etc. But beware: It is not the fixture that provides the solution, but rather how it is applied.

This process should occur prior to schematic design. All spaces must be considered simultaneously, not done one at a time, which guards against all spaces having the same solution. Along these lines, each space needs to be described individually, whether in words or drawings, to guarantee individual solutions.

Schematic design: focus on concept

As schematic design commences, a lighting comparison of all spaces should begin in concept. As schematic design

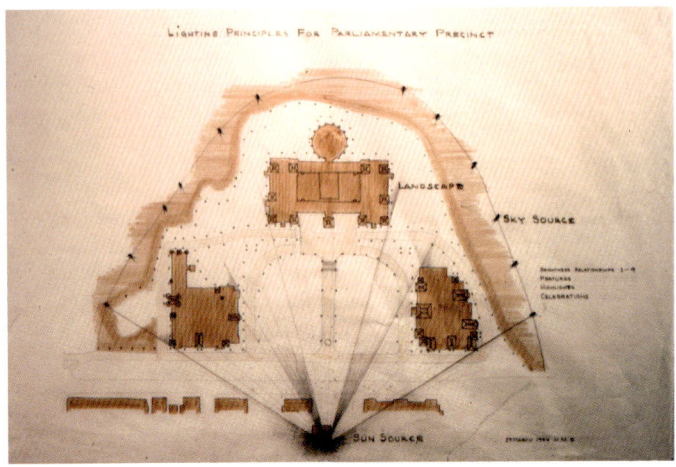

Figure 12-2. **Ottawa Parliamentary Precinct: hand-drawn conceptual sketch of lighting scheme.**

nears completion, this concept should be well developed. When the visual hierarchy or itinerary through the project is set and each space is lighted in a manner that will result in the way both the user and designer want it to look, then all lighting and control equipment can be selected. When this selection is concluded, a complete lighting quantification should occur. Major projects require calculations of surround, local and background illuminances. Most projects, however, can use simple rule-of-thumb calculations. Supplementary lights should then be added if required for any tasks. Adjustments should then be made (during design development) to ensure that all program goals have been met, including meeting the budget. When this is completed, there is at least the potential for a high-quality lighting system.

> Shadow control is an important element of every project—as when capturing a photo where key light is the sun, and fill light is the sky.

Now let's do it! Focus on construction

- A good set of working drawings that accurately locates each light fixture and its focus, and clearly indicates its type

Peter Boyce, Professor Emeritus of Architecture, Rensselaer Polytechnic Institute

It is a cliché that lighting is both an art and a science, but it is also a cause of conflict. At the extremes of this conflict are the stereotyped designer and scientist. Put crudely, stereotyped scientists believe that designers are essentially mountebanks who will claim anything if it helps them win a commission. Conversely, stereotyped designers believe that scientists are aesthetically challenged nerds who would not recognize a thing of beauty if it fell on them. The question I wish to address is how these extremes might be reconciled. My reason for doing so is simply that unless the art and science of lighting can be reconciled, many opportunities will be lost. Designers will miss out on the understanding provided by science, and scientists will be unaware of the insights of designers.

The starting point for any reconciliation is to admit that there really are people representative of the two stereotypes amongst both designers and scientists. Such people are characterized by an arrogant temperament and a closed mind. But there are also some who are more humble and more open-minded. There are designers who are willing to make the effort to understand the science of lighting, and there are scientists who are willing to listen to designers, to learn why they do what they do. Following the open mind is more likely to be rewarding than crouching behind the barriers erected by the closed mind, with one proviso—the open mind should not be an empty mind. Rather, it should be an inquiring mind. One characteristic of an inquiring mind is recognition of the value of experience, but only useful experience. Experience as a simple passage of time has no value. It is experience that involves close observation and analysis that is of value. Careful observation combined with curiosity is the starting point of both design and science. Cuttle argues that lighting design is essentially a three-step process: observation, visualization and realization. For science, the steps are observation, hypothesis generation, experimentation and replication. But where do designers and scientists carry out their observations? Many lighting designers start their observations in the theatre. The problem with this is that the theatre is a special place where disbelief is often suspended. In many ways, the experience of the effects of lighting in the theatre is similar to a proof of concept study in the laboratory. In both locations, extreme conditions are used to ensure an effect. With this background, the question that naturally arises is how generalizable are the conclusions drawn from observations made in the theatre when applied to more mundane situations. From what we know now, it appears that simple perceptions such as brightness and color are reliably transferred, but predictions made about more complex perceptions and emotions that are influenced by the context in which they occur are much less reliable. As for the scientist, the conditions used in laboratory experiments are often extremely simplified in order to control significant variables, but such control eradicates many phenomena of interest. Again, how generalizable are the conclusions drawn from observations made in simplified laboratory studies when applied to more complex situations? In this case, what we know now suggests that phenomena that are based on the operation of the human visual system can be reliably transferred to the real world, but perceptions that depend on context are much more uncertain.

Although an inquiring mind is a necessary condition for appreciating both the art and science of lighting, it is not sufficient. It is also necessary to appreciate that both designers and scientists have something to contribute to our understanding of lighting. Designers should be a copious source of material for scientists. In many ways, every completed design can be regarded as an experiment. The problem is that they are never treated as such. The designer rarely states exactly what the predicted effects of the proposed lighting design will be and the outcome is even more rarely evaluated so as to test those predictions. Scientists could be a useful source of techniques for carrying out such evaluations, as well as compendiums of knowledge about the visual and non-visual effects of light.

But simply recognizing what might be gained from listening to each other is still not enough. What is also required is a willingness to abandon old habits. For designers, this means recognizing that while belief may be enough for religion, it is not enough for science. For science, some evidence is required, based on either the literature of the subject or on measurement, before asserts can be accepted. For scientists, it means recognizing the fact that if there is no evidence to support an assertion that does not mean the assertion is wrong, but rather that it is unproven and should be treated as a hypothesis to be tested.

If both designers and scientists interested in lighting could be persuaded to move from a position of mutual incomprehension and suspicion to one of cooperation, it would contribute much to the effective evolution of lighting practice. For many years, the vast majority of lighting installations have been designed simply to ensure adequate visual performance without visual discomfort, but this is changing. Today, more and more building owners and users are willing to take a holistic view of the value of lighting, a value that encompasses the effect of lighting on perceptions, behavior and health as well as performance and comfort. Designers have experience in creating lighting to meet these objectives. Scientists have the expertise to measure how well these objectives have been met. Designers and scientists working together will make progress further and faster than working separately.

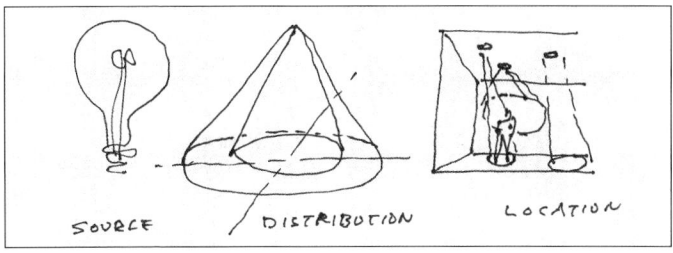

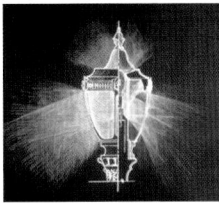

Figure 12-3. Examples of the Lighting Design Process: the plan for Battery Park City, from conceptual sketches while pondering the activity in the area (top), to fixture design (left) to implementation (right).

- A comprehensive set of specifications that leaves no doubt as to the photometric properties of the fixture, its distribution and viewed photometric brightness, etc.
- A thorough review of the shop drawings submitted to determine whether or not everything required in the specification is provided
- Careful field observation of the installation in progress to verify compliance with the location, lamping and focus as specified in the working drawings
- Conduct a Post-Occupancy Evaluation to determine the extent to which the installed lighting system met the project goals. Make adjustments as required.

One more step must be taken. The user's maintenance and purchasing personnel must be present during the design process so they understand it thoroughly and are motivated to service it properly. Without their cooperation, there is little hope of the lighting continuing to function as designed for the life of the project.

Finally, the job is not complete until a Post-Occupancy Evaluation survey has been done. Similar to the subjective analysis described earlier, this feedback process ensures that knowledge continues to grow and enables the advances of lighting's contribution to the future needs of the project or new work.

It takes at least this degree of effort to provide good professional lighting design services or to successfully complete any design projects life presents to you. Below is a brief summary of all the steps outlined.

Summing it up

- Review the user's program.
- Visit selected facilities and then the client's existing site to establish a design vocabulary and project objectives, including budgets.
- Compose a visual hierarchy for all spaces and an itinerary through them.
- Light each space appropriately for appearance.
- Supplement for task requirements.
- Evaluate the total design.
- Prepare a budget.
- Prepare bid documents.
- Meticulously check shop drawings and installation.
- Involve and instruct user's personnel in the system.
- Perform a Post-Occupancy Evaluation.

Make it a practice to light the space first, then supplement for the individual tasks if required.

And always, always write it down. If it isn't in writing, it doesn't exist!

13
Write It Down

"One needs an open mind and great ego control to do good work. There is a difference between pride and ego; most people do not have the patience to understand this. They are either too selfish or self-centered."
—the author

ALMOST AS IMPORTANT AS LEARNING TO SEE is learning to communicate. The following quote illustrates the importance of developing your own system of writing lighting. Sir Edwin Landseer Luytens, the English architect who planned New Delhi, said, "Those idiotic diagrams which architects and others make don't work. Light is like a flood, and you might as well try to show the banks of a river, its flows and varying depths, swirls, eddies and currents with one arrow." There is essentially no thought given to lighting by most planners and even less given to lighting in their education. Is lighting taught in, or even a part of, urban planning curriculum? I don't believe so. Hence we see how abominably our cities are lighted under most city planning guidelines.

The quality of your life depends on your ability to communicate. Regardless of how many projects you've done or places you have occupied, or how similar they are, by definition, no two can be alike. Communication between user and designer is critical in achieving a good lighting design (or anything else for that matter); it is important, therefore, to use more than one method when explaining lighting and design or anything else: Speak! Write! Draw! These are the three effective methods of communication.

> Writing lighting ... Do you think about lighting? When you do, how do you measure the thought? How many light meter measurements do you make a day? How do you take them? Do you have a check for brightness, direction and power of the light in the area, the general lighting or other aspects of the lighting you are viewing? Do you have a method for writing that down, like a musician or choreographer does?

Consider how Edgar Allen Poe in "The Fall of the House of Usher" describes a room so perfectly you can easily picture you are there, immersed in its atmosphere:

> The room in which I found myself was very large and lofty. The windows were long, narrow and pointed, and at so vast a distance from the black oaken floor as to be altogether inaccessible from within. Feeble gleams of encrimsoned light made their way through the trellised panes, and served to render sufficiently distinct the more prominent objects around; the eye,

Figure 13-1. Computer renderings. To aid in "seeing," there are several tools available: light meter, spectroscope, computer software. Remember: They are just tools. Lighting designers have to learn to communicate what the client is going to get at the end, what it is they are going to "see." The best criticism at the end of a project: "This looks exactly as you told me it would." That is what you are attempting to do. It takes several communication skills: spoken word, written word, drawings, mockups, computer renderings, etc. Computer renderings may be the most sterile of the methods you can use. Think about it: An image on a screen or a printout is all you'll be able to offer. Can it adequately express the emotion—the life—of the project?

however, struggled in vain to reach the remoter angles of the chamber, or the recesses of the vaulted and fretted ceiling. Dark draperies hung upon the walls. The general furniture was profuse, comfortless, antique and tattered. Many books and musical instruments lay scattered about, but failed to give any vitality to the scene. I felt that I breathed an atmosphere of sorrow. An air of stern, deep and irredeemable gloom hung over and pervaded all.

The Lighting Design Process graphic in Chapter 12 demonstrates an alternate way of clearly communicating all the preceding lists in a visual format.

Figure 13-2. What is truth? What you see or what you measure? The man above is wearing glasses with yellow lenses; understandably, he sees things as very much brighter, yet his meter registers a lower number than that of the sun. Which appears brighter to the man? Leonardo da Vinci provides a hint: "All our knowledge has its origins in our perceptions." What you see is the truth!

In essence, a designer is a salesperson. Your skill as a designer relies heavily on your ability to be a good salesperson—to sell your ideas both to yourself and the prospective users. Paint a picture for them starting from the broadest possible perspective. This is an extremely important element in developing a way of thinking.

> Drawing is putting your mind on paper for other people to see. Every bit of work you do, even a sketch, has to be considered as a work of art; it is a measure of your morality and social conscience, with every new piece of work being a new reality.

14
Lighting the Lady

"For me, light is a pilgrimage. It is the soul of the desire that drives me to create."
—the author

IN REVIEW, LIGHT IS THE PATH to what it is you wish to see. Light is a pure form of energy that is neutral to all matter it touches no matter what the context. It is an essential natural energy that is produced in many ways. Lighting is the application of light to compose space. It is a malleable medium that manipulates the senses to reinforce the context and mood of spaces. Lighting is an art unto itself, supported and enhanced by science.

Lighting the Lady is a perfect illustration of these concepts.

When our firm learned that we had been chosen to design the lighting for the restored Statue of Liberty, we knew that this project demanded more than the careful application of our professional skills. It was the centennial of France's gift of Lady Liberty to the United States to commemorate the American Revolution. This is a very special monument. It has meaning not only to Americans, but to people the world over.

And so, as we began our involvement with the Statue, we were constantly operating on two levels. As a lighting project, it presented many of the same problems we had found in lighting hundreds of other public places, like parks, libraries, offices and hotels. But, on a totally different plane, lighting Liberty created a greater slew of emotions within us than had ever existed on any other project. Our sense of pride expanded, of course, but so did our awareness of the scope of our responsibility. The structural restoration of the Statue for its hundredth anniversary would need to last for at least another century. If we did our job right, the illumination would last as long.

The formal name of this great monument is "Liberty Enlightening the World," but throughout much of its history, the hopes of those charged with lighting this great lady were limited by the existing technology at the time.

At first, beams of light were supposed to stream from her crown. The construction engineer suggested bright lights at the pedestal, too. Holes were cut into the copper sheeting around the torch and lamps were installed inside. Nothing really worked well. The light from the torch caused a shadow that obscured the Statue's shoulders and head. The base lights failed to illuminate the monument. When Bertholdi visited his work in September 1893, he expressed great disappointment with the lighting and suggested that the solution might be to gild the entire statue. There was no solution until 1915, when George Williams, an electrical engineer, who shared Bertholdi's concern, came up with a design for lighting the Statue and the General Electric Company (GE) provided the new technology to realize the design, and fulfill the vision for that moment.

When we came on board, even more advanced technology would enable us do the job right. We could make this symbol to the world look good. What did that simple goal—making it look good—mean? To us, it meant that the lighting must reveal this work of art, give it form, maintain its dignity and compose its setting in the harbor.

It did *not* mean that it should be a lighting *tour de force*. It did not mean that it should be a theatrical event. That would denigrate this magnificent symbol. There are moments when dramatic lighting is appropriate, but the day-to-day illumination of an international symbol isn't one of them. Making this great lady look good also did not mean that we simply find new ways to throw the greatest amount of light on this monument and wash it all in a dazzling blaze. With light everywhere—all pervasive and omnipresent as in a fog—an object simply gets lost. Our mission was to light the Statue as a work of art, not to treat it as a floodlighting contract.

> I pondered the challenge of how to illuminate this icon, so I took a boat out into the harbor and observed her from various distances and at every angle. I observed her at dawn, noon, dusk and in the darkness of night. At some point in the process, I walked to the end of the Battery Park Promenade, sat on a stone wall, and it came to me: She looked best in the light of dawn. I took out my little notepad and wrote: "Needed: one light source with spectral power distribution to mimic the morning sun, one to mimic the morning sky and a new light fixture to project light from a great distance—this will make a lady with green skin look good."

No rules for lighting a green lady...

When you begin to design light to give form to a work of art, standard references must be tossed aside. Standards are not acceptable for something unique. Doing this job right meant paying great attention to minute details, making repeated close observations. Calculations were merely tools to determine whether it was likely one had made a mistake. The uniqueness of this commission was multi-fold and daunting. The lady in question:

- represents the greatest symbol of freedom to the most people at any time in history;
- is seen at all hours of the day and night from all vantage points in New York Harbor and beyond, to the surrounding sites of New York City, New Jersey and Staten Island;
- is visible to every ship sailing in from any domestic or foreign port on any given day;
- leaves passengers in awe as they fly in to Newark, LaGuardia and JFK every day of the year; and
- is green!

She took "high visibility" to new heights. We capitalized on the fact that we had a full-size mockup—the Statue itself. We believed that nothing short of a full-size mockup would be effective to test this lighting and give us an absolute reference point.

Notably, the 150-foot copper monument had succumbed to the oxidation of time and elements by which she was surrounded. Behold; she is green. The intricacies of her structure flowed one into the next, from her solid stance on that massive fort to the undulations in her robe; from the splay of her pages to the spikes in her crown and the tongues of her flame. The torch that she carries is visible not just from New York Harbor, but in the hearts of people in the far most reaches of the world. The book she carries could be read by torchlight when it got dark. The symbolism was not lost on us. We were able to control and turn light on to see whenever we needed, reading being the indispensable building block of freedom.

Composing the vision

Before all the scaffolding went up, we photographed the monument from every conceivable angle, including every section of fold in the robe, every segment of the pedestal and fort. We looked carefully and made precise angle and location measurements from every spot on the island. We viewed the statue from boats, from surrounding buildings, from roads around the harbor. We examined every potential spot where it seemed light should be used to reveal Bertholdi's work.

Next we considered all the available light sources that could be used on the project and, just as important, ways to simplify maintenance by the National Park Service. That meant going through countless catalogs and taking boatloads of fixtures out to the statue to try. We also made a careful evaluation of the light sources used in the 1976 lighting redesign.

We made an important discovery and uncovered a major problem. Manufacturers really did not make light sources that flatter green ladies. Green she was, and green she

Figure 14-1.
Gil Reiling of GE, inventor of the metal halide lamp (left), and the author on Liberty Island.

would remain. The lights that were available would have made the figure look too dramatic or too muddy.

It was clear to us that Lady Liberty looked best in dawn's early light. During the early morning hours, the statue looks her most radiant, and therefore most moving. The position of her arm, the book she was holding and the torch were all enhanced by the morning light. With that inspiration, we devised a means to replicate dawn. This would require two lamps, each with a wholly new color output. GE worked with us to develop the two new metal halide lamps that produced just the right effect on the green surface patina. One lamp mimicked the light of the morning sun, producing the warmer component that would illuminate the highlights, while the other mimicked the light of the blue sky in the early morning—the cooler component to fill in the folds and shadows.

Remember, our goal was the lighting of the torch—a problem from the time the monument was constructed. Until 1916, the torch bore little resemblance to Bertholdi's vision of a monument to "Liberty Enlightening the World." It barely glowed. The 1916 reconstruction produced the torch as we have all grown to recognize it: yellowish cathedral glass held together by a steel frame and lit from within.

We believed that the newly restored torch would be a blaze of glory that finally realized Bertholdi's dream. The torch would be covered with gilt—implementing the suggestion Bertholdi made in 1893—that would glitter in the sun during the day and become lighted at night to a brilliant intensity. The result was no guesswork. We hung gold foil over the torch and evaluated it by day, and then lighted it by night, until we achieved the desired result—the one that looked good.

Determining the visual hierarchy

Illuminating this national treasure could not be done properly unless the design was sensitive to the overall composition—the monument in its harbor setting. When the Statue of Liberty was first erected, it was the tallest structure in the harbor. There was also very little lighting on the shoreline. Now, buildings in Manhattan tower above it and because of the abundance of ambient light in the area, the Statue would be visible even if it were not illuminated at all.

We felt the lighting had to give the monument a stronger presence in the harbor and to create, as much as possible, a sense of its dominance and height. Dividing a project's brightness beyond four, I have found, is rarely required. For Lady Liberty, we decided which areas of the statue we wanted to see range from brightest to dimmest, from one to four, then noted how much contrast the scene yielded via its materials. In our design, therefore, the figure did not suddenly emerge in a blaze of light out of the darkness of the water. Instead, we begin to softly light the fort, light the pedestal a bit brighter and the hem of the skirt even brighter, and then bring the level of illumination to a crescendo as we move toward the top. There, the brightest lights of all would be located in the crown and torch, drawing one's eye upward and to its destination (see Figure 14-2).

> Luminance ratios are used by some people as a part of the assessment and/or planning of a lighting system. I just use my years of experience. There are so many other factors that come into play that following preset luminance ratios may be a quick route to a series of spaces that look so similar as to create boredom. It is easy to do lighting design that way because it eliminates thinking about project requirements. Although it does require a bit of calculation, you merely have to fill the luminance ratio prescription—another thought-free solution.

The lighting design would produce a greater sense of

Figure 14-2. The hierarchy of brilliance is established, softest—just a hint of light—at the base to give context to the Lady's place in the dark waters of New York Harbor, then gradually increasing in intensity to draw your gaze upward to the pinnacle, glowing brightest at the crown and the torch, the ultimate focal points.

height without the effect of an overpowering hulk rising mysteriously out of the darkness of the sea. It would simply reveal a welcoming presence in the harbor entrance. A light in the window at home: Homeland.

Homelands have their celebrations, of course, and so we made provision for some spectacular lighting for special occasions. Then, and only then, we proposed that beams of light would stream from the crown thousands of feet up into the sky. Moreover, to enhance its effect and increase the visibility of the lighting, we suggested that wisps of vapor should emerge from the torch.

GE began manufacturing the new lamps; we planned to supervise their installation the following spring. We would observe, test, evaluate, adjust and check again. We would continue to work with the dedication and hope that what we did would last for the next 100 years and produce a better view of our lady in the harbor.

Putting it all together

I relied on my ability to "see" to bring our vision to light, in this case reinforced by my time-lapse sense memory observing the Lady from earliest morning to pitch black of

Figure 14-3. Lighting the Lady. © PETER B. KAPLAN 1986, ALL RIGHTS RESERVED COURTESY PETER B. KAPLAN IMAGES, INC (3) WWW.PETERBKAPLANSTOCK.COM.

night. As Stanislavski said, you can't experience everything, so draw on your closest memory to recreate it.

The idea was not to change the appearance of the statue, but to make her look her best at all hours of the day and night. From my observations, the particular color quality of dawn and early morning were most flattering. I had tried countless fixtures, took boatloads of existing lamps out there, and none worked. It was time to breed new light sources using our knowledge of science to support the art. Figure 14-4 illustrates that knowing the science allows us to

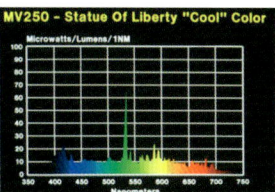

Figure 14-4.

Arc tube and spectral power distribution of "cool" metal halide lamp to mimic the morning sky.

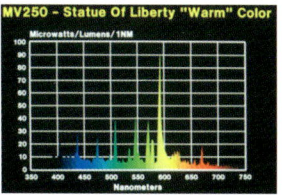

Arc tube and spectral power distribution of "warm" metal halide lamp to mimic the morning sun.

create the art to evoke the emotion. We sidestepped a comfort zone—out of the bounds of recommended practice—unafraid to declare what was not there and develop it. After all, design based on fear is not design.

15
Illuminating History, Education and Ceremony

"For any man-made place, the spaces are the melody and the lighting is the orchestration. To advance lighting design, the message has to be an ostanato to architecture."
—the author

IN 1994, THE BRANDSTON PARTNERSHIP developed the lighting concept for the renovation of St. Meinrad's Archabbey, a Benedictine monastery in the little town of St. Meinrad, located in the hills of southern Indiana.

Pope Pius XII bestowed the name of "Archabbey" on Saint Meinrad during its centennial in 1954 to honor its role in the development of Benedictine monasteries in the United States. St. Meinrad's is one of nine archabbeys in the world and one of only two in the United States. Here reside 120 monks who run a graduate school for Roman Catholic priesthood and host year-round retreats. It is a place of history, education and ceremony.

There are still many places in the world that have changed very little. Some are now preserved by landmark status. That is the important consideration. We need a sense of the light of contemporary life of past centuries. It helps us to deal with the lighting in our time. When change is required, however, the responsible alteration, when done, should not intrude on what was previously built.

The lighting for the renovation of the St. Meinrad Archabbey is easily understood when we consider the following. Whatever mystery seems to enshroud lighting can be lifted as easily as a veil if one only considers the spaces being illuminated and where it is appropriate for the light to be placed. All you need to do is to decide which one of these spaces you wish people to see first and make it the brightest area. You continue in the same manner until all spaces have been placed in a hierarchical order of consideration and brightness. Oftentimes, there are different uses for each space that may change the lighting needs, and therefore the hierarchical order previously determined. Then, all you need to do is to plan for a means to change the brightness of that space. The same holds true for both the outside and the inside of building.

Inside spaces

We will start the description of the proposed lighting system by imagining we have entered the building late on a sunny summer morning. There are no electric lamps or candles lighted. The sun is warming the north wall, its light tinted as it passes through stained glass windows. The east, west and south walls are not black, nor is the ceiling or the floor, for they are lighted by the multiple reflections from the first surface being lighted. As the time of day passes and the sun's position changes until it is gone, the evanescence of this daily, seasonal event

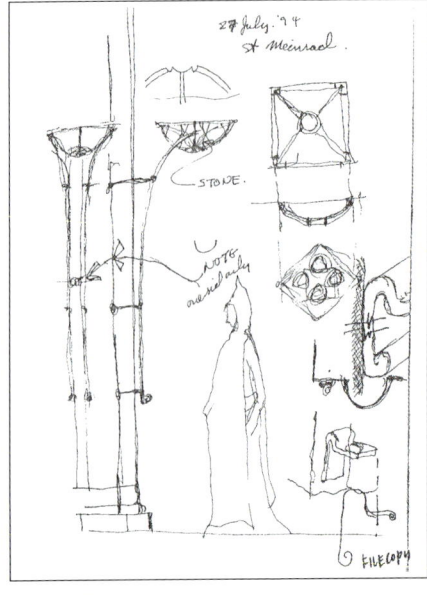

Figure 15-1.

could, with study, be committed to one's memory.

The above description is the beginning point of the lighting design. Designed lighting is the intervention, by means of electric and candlelight, to modify the environment given from the daylight and to serve our needs within the building. We begin the process by adding layers of light on the various surfaces of the spaces and objects and people, including hymnals, so that every use can be appropriately illuminated to be seen.

We see those layers, and the means to deliver the required lighting, in no hierarchical order, as depicted in the preliminary concept sketches shown here.

All the vaults in the nave will be lighted from column mounted torchières. Wall brackets will be used to provide lighting in the vaults where torchières cannot be used.

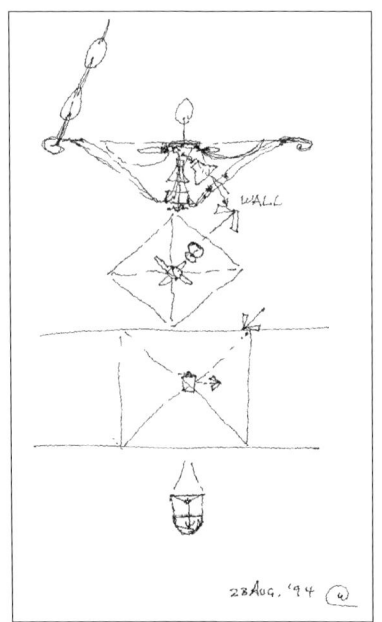 

Figure 15-2.

All the vaults in the aisles will be lighted by an uplight component of a suspended chandelier that will also glow softly. An additional spotlamp concealed in the fixture will gently light the wall and part of the floor.

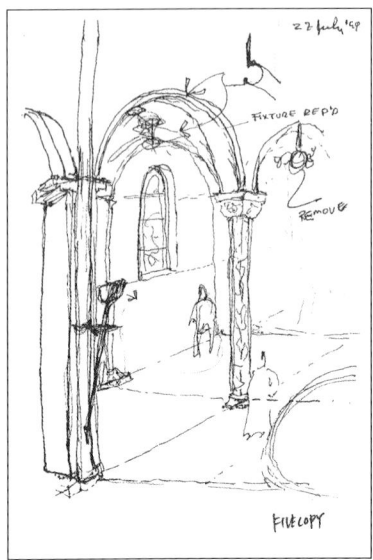

Figure 15-3.

The floor will be illuminated by groups of focusable lights recessed in the ceiling at the center of the ornament in the vaults of the nave.

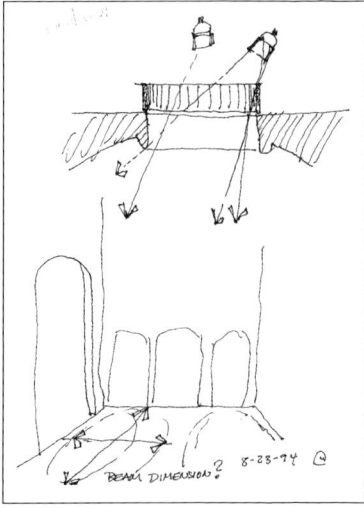

Figure 15-4.

Selected spotlamps in the focusable recessed lights will be used to highlight objects or function areas within the church. Some of these areas will be the altar and the surrounding ceremonial area, President's chair, organ pipes, etc.

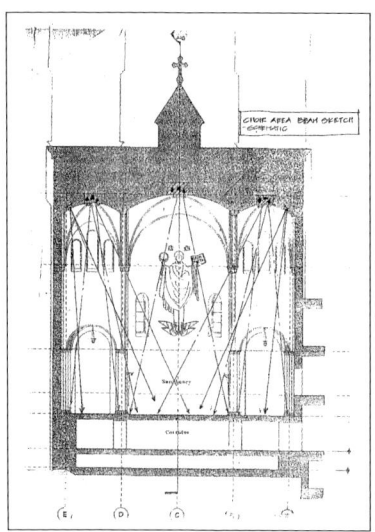

Figure 15-5.

Accent lights, sufficient for people of all ages, will light the choir to assist in reading. These fixtures will be located high on the walls of the newly formed transept. A special "candle" lamp will be positioned on the choir stalls to add a focal glow to the area.

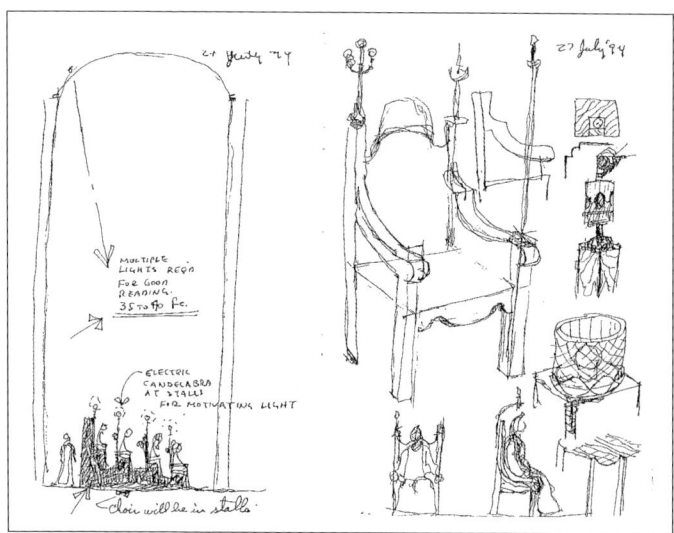

Figure 15-6.

Adjustable fixtures will light the walls of the apse and the room formed by the new location of the organ pipes. These will be located at the top of the vault above and behind the columns that delineate the apse.

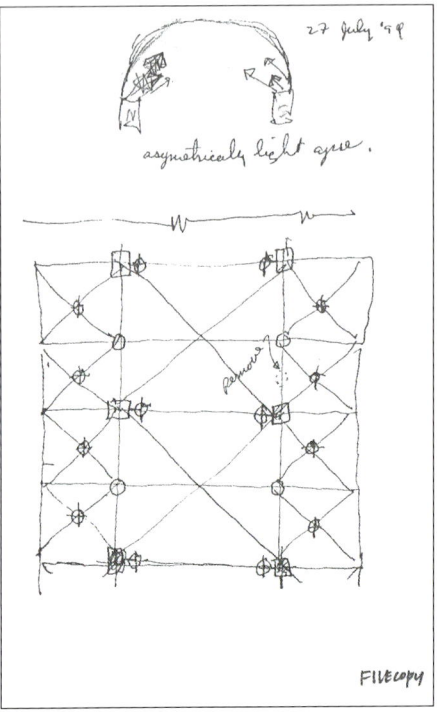

Figure 15-7.

Outside spaces

Again, as above, create for yourself a daytime seasonal sense memory of the appearance of the church. With this "sense" in mind, we began the lighting design by considering what parts of the church we wished to be able to see after the sun had set.

We believed that a glow should have encompassed the northern side of the building and the towers that was just slightly brighter than the light of the full moon. The sources to provide this glow could be mounted on poles hidden in the trees that bordered the pathway to the northwest.

Summary

The above narrative is a description of the ideas that we gathered on our site visit to the Archabbey on 26 July 1994. Those notions were blended and tempered by our experience at St. Bede's, another Benedictine Monastery in Peru, Illinois; as well as work we completed on other houses of worship. It was meant as a supplement to aid in the understanding of the schematic drawings included in this submission at that time. Another purpose was to encourage constructive criticism and thinking about the visual hierarchy of the spaces and the variety of change that may have been required for the ceremonies that the lighting would have to serve. We looked forward to the response. The process, as always, was interactive, with *communication* at the heart of it every time.

The ability to "see" derives from a sort of subliminal awareness of previous experiences, sensations and memories stored, to be drawn upon another day.

Do you "see" or are you only a "looker"?

16
A Grand Vision for Detroit

"Gio Ponti said, 'The architect's duty is to interpret a community to itself.' But I would go beyond that and say that the architect's burden is to interpret a community to the world." —the author

THE LIGHTING MASTER PLAN for Detroit's business district demonstrates that light is a city's lifeblood, and also demonstrates the value for communities to take responsibility for their lighting and not leave it to public departments, so as to receive optimal benefit from light.

When Brandston Partnership received an RFP to develop a lighting master plan for the central business district in downtown Detroit, our first response was that the RFP, issued by Detroit's Central Business District Association, was naïve and unattainable.

Our second response: We rewrote the RFP to make it achievable, more holistic and produce a better result. We submitted a response to our version.

The Association told us we didn't get the job, but that they were going to resend the RFP—our version, as they liked it better. At this time, I started to feel that being based outside of Detroit would be a detriment to our firm. But we responded to the new RFP. The next time the Association called, it was to tell us they still liked our response the best. They hired a Detroit-based consultant who engaged us in an interview process and recommended our firm. We got the job.

Our task was to produce a master plan, a guideline for development of the district's lighting. We worked with a local architectural/engineering firm to assist with local work. Local design firms would realize the concept.

The first step was research, a major component of Brandston Partnership's approach. After all, you can't think about something you know nothing about. In a designer's work for a client, about 40 percent of the value is the preliminary study.

Hayden McKay, our project manager, and I went to Detroit and studied vehicle and foot traffic patterns, and how the districts were used. We walked every street. We viewed the city from the vantage point of a helicopter so we could see more clearly where people congregated, and when. We photographed everything.

By the end, we had measured the pulse of Detroit and had watched it breathe.

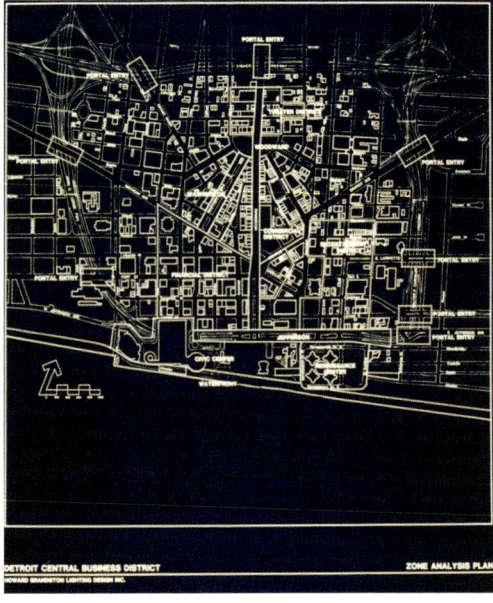

Figure 16-1.
Detroit Central Business District.

Our next step was to use this data to divide the city into districts based on their use, and developed our own district plan based on this. We noted that Detroit is indeed the "motor city," being cut into several sections by major roadways. This revealed the real fabric of the street scene in Detroit. We also found that the District was really a parking lot. A significant portion of the area was outdoor parking lots, with few parks and almost no green view. We also made a sketch to show the scale of the city.

The result was a plan that, once realized, would become one of the major urban lighting projects of the world.

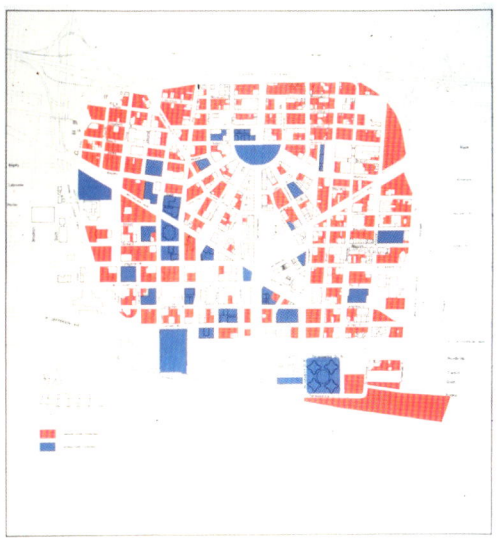

Figure 16-2.
A city of parking lots.
The red-shaded areas represent outdoor open parking lots.
The blue-shaded areas represent buildings with internal parking facilities.

The plan would provide a grander view of the city, make life more comfortable by prompting wayfinding and pathfinding via landmarks, provide a unique identity to the district and create a real urban setting by lighting major ways like streets instead of highways. It was first and foremost a holistic solution.

Major roadways served as arteries entering the central business district; we identified these entry points as portals, and recommended relighting these points with decorative post fixtures.

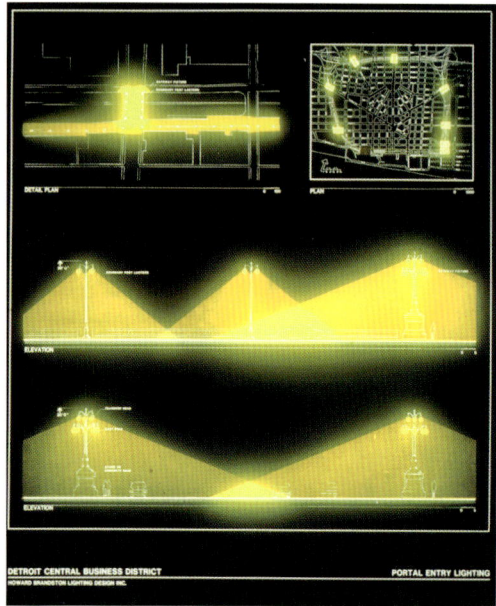

Figure 16-3. Major roadways served as arteries entering the central business district; Brandston Partnership identified these entry points as portals, and recommended relighting these points with decorative fixtures.

Key landmark buildings would be lighted uniquely to make them more visible and develop a unique character that would be easily recognizable, which in turn would become part of the wayfinding solution. We developed a list of all historic buildings, monuments, houses of worship and other notable buildings to determine how to fit them into the lighting scheme and promote wayfinding.

The entire district's public lighting, typically comprised of utilitarian high-pressure sodium fixtures, would be replaced with metal halide fixtures to produce a white light that distinguished the district from the rest of the city.

Lighting would also be used to create a central artery separating the parks, waterfront, sports, recreation and cultural activity areas from the main body of the business district. Decorative fixtures would be used on this main drag as well as in the parks to distinguish these areas from the rest of the business district.

The waterfront lighting was modeled on the Victoria Embankment on the Thames River in London, patterned with special decorative fixtures to make the area pedestrian-friendly, as this area—like the parks and main drag—received significant foot traffic.

As the plan became implemented, all of the identified landmarks, parks and important places were brought to life through light. The major arteries feeding the district became beautiful again.

During the process of developing the master plan, I was asked if I wanted to consult with the department of Parks, Transportation, Electricity, Police, etc. I said of course, but only after the plan was completed; I did not wish to be a referee of turf wars that could only weaken the plan and derail its implementation.

Mayor Coleman Young accepted this and added: Get it done. The public departments hated the plan. The client loved it.

The private sector spent millions to execute our plan and recompose their nightscape. The result was nothing less than extraordinary as Detroit became transformed through light.

17
Learning to See: An Emotional Response

"Information comes from books, references, teachers. Knowledge comes from experience. Work to build knowledge."
—the author

HAVE YOU HEARD THE NAME ALHAZEN? Most people haven't. A name virtually unknown amongst the great thinkers, his contribution to optics and physics as we know and understand them is so intricately entwined in us that we don't recognize it as an innovation. Yet with a single observation, this ancient Arab scientist, born Abu Ali al-Hasan Ibn al-Haytham around the year 965, put to rest an 800-year-old debate and solved the mystery of vision.

Two theories battled to explain how we see. Mathematicians, Euclid and Ptolemy among them, were convinced that light traveled from the eye to objects we observed. The atomists, including Aristotle, believed the opposite, that light entered the eye from an external source. Ptolemy's theory was rooted in math and reason, while Aristotle's was mostly conjecture, but the completeness and consistency of both theories left little room to question either. Ibn al-Haytham relied on observation. He asked spectators to stare at the sun! What could be simpler? Naturally, looking at such a bright object burned the eye. Neither geometry nor theory could compete with his data; the evidence showed that light began outside the eye and reflected into it. Direct observation became a way to know the world, and experimentation and observation transformed life for the next thousand years (Richard Powers, *The New York Times Magazine*, 1999).

Despite Alhazen's demonstration to the contrary, perhaps the ancient Greeks' idea that light shot out of the eye like sparks, touching objects, had its truth. For it is the inner light of our body that provides learned sight, though you would never know it based on how much we rely on technology today.

Cell phones have become a fifth appendage, with newborns practically the only sect of our species not under their spell. Design happens at the speed of a mouse these days, with computer drawing programs, lighting simulations that attempt to portray a "realistic" rendering of light in a space and lighting calculation programs that eliminate the need to multiply or divide with that relic of a handheld calculator anymore. All this technology is but the anatomical skeleton of a lighting design system. As we all know, there's no homogenized person. Despite some skeletal framework, when you put it all together, it ends up different. Clearly, just as bones do not make the person, neither do technical pieces make up a lighting design that is deeply satisfying in human terms. Therefore, technology in a design culture must be taught by showing the structural role this component of lighting plays in a design. This should be done by starting with an example of a project, illustrating the end result of the lighting and then dissecting out the part each component played in achieving the illuminated composition.

We can overdesign too easily, when simplicity and attention to the immediate objective is all that is required. A system for achieving any objective should be tailored to the realities of the problem. Case in point: an Olympic rifleman's objective is to place all the bullets through one hole without regard for the distance. Realistically, this caliber of competitor and equipment can obtain sub minute of angle accuracy or, to put it simply, place 10 bullets in one-half of a standard postage stamp at 100 yards. The successful big-game hunter, on the other hand, has no need for such precision. If we attempt to impose a one-size-fits-all solution to all hunters, we fail miserably. Trying to inflict the Olympian's criteria on the big-game hunter is misplaced and poor design. All that is needed is a readily understandable metric to evaluate the potential task, nothing more.

Application is the assembly of all the parts of the anatomy, bringing a lighting design to life. It demands the ability to visualize what each technical component contributes to the body of the work and then assemble it into a system. Again, this education starts with a design and what it is that the particular lighting system wishes you to see and why. A sifting-through process commences and continues until the body of the work is a lighted whole.

By now, you must be tired of hearing my musings, but I must tug at your shirt sleeve one last time: Preconceived ideas for a project set a bias which becomes a paradigm that in turn eliminates fresh thinking and prohibits a design from setting its own course. Make a difference—a measurable delta—that is memorable. That is where my imperative lies.

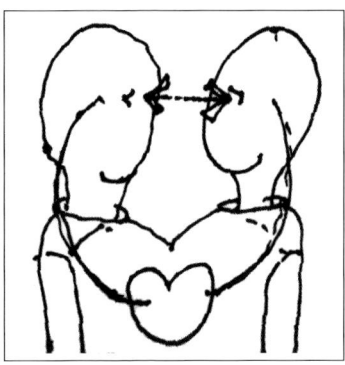

Figure 17-1.
Light is a subconscious element of design in any space which can evoke any given emotional response.

Recall Cyrano de Bergerac, that touching yet tragic character created by poet Edmond Rostand in the eponymous 1897 play. Cyrano, a valiant swordsman and eloquent poet saddled with a hideous nose, was deeply in love with his beautiful and intellectual cousin, Roxane, who in turn was in love with the handsome Christian. Cyrano offered to write words of love to substitute for those of his less articulate friend, Christian, in Christian's plight to woo Roxane, thus allowing Cyrano to express his feelings without revealing himself and risking rejection. Even after Roxane and Christian married, Cyrano continued to be his voice for many years. In the end, as Cyrano became wounded and neared death, Roxane realized that he was the soul she had been in love with all those years, that the words that touched her heart were his—not the one whose visage was more appealing but whose being was devoid of substance.

Just as appearance without emotion is empty, lighting without emotion is sterile. And that emotional response is defined by the culture that surrounds you—culture being your country, region or even corporate environment. These evaluations are formed but are subject to the influences around you—the people and climate that affect your preferences, and your sentiments. It is the responsibility of a designer to awaken sensitivity to that emotion because that emotion is part of your life. Imagine a kitchen in Mexico, for example. It would most likely be filled with colorful pottery, pungent spices and passionate voices at a dinner table. Now step into a kitchen in Scandinavia; it conjures up a very different picture: tailored furnishings, cooler aesthetic, softer colors, milder flavorings—no less beautiful, but a complete contrast in appearance and substance. Culture.

Lighting, our exemplary design example throughout this book, is primarily an art, an art supported by science. Therefore, any work based on science, technology and recommended practice alone will, at best, be ordinary. Stay openminded, listen, see and understand—for the tyranny of discipline can render you myopic. Lighting requires not only our curiosity, but our ability to make subjective evaluations as well. We should know how to test those subjective evaluations to make sure we are narrowing down the choices to the one that has the most probability of being successful. Learning to "see" has an enormous subjective component to it—it's that emotional response that completes the connection—yielding our ultimate reward: self-confidence.

Appendices

Appendix I
Explanation of Popular Lighting Terms

Glare

How often have you held your hand up to your eye to shield from glare? Or caught a flash out of the corner of your eye? Something too bright? Something that you would refer to as glary? Have you ever thought about why an object or light source appears to cause glare?

Glare is the contrast of a brightly lighted area adjacent to a darker area. It is that degree of brightness due to contrast that is noticeable—often dramatic, sometimes intentional, sometimes uncomfortable. Glare is a component of light and therefore naturally of lighting design. Glare is not always a bad thing: On the contrary, depending on cultural origin, preferences or situations, glare may be perceived as good (uniformity, in fact, is the watchword of uninteresting design). Of course, there are degrees of glare, ranging from "sparkle," which can be attractive and desirable; to discomfort glare, which is mildly to strongly irritating but tolerable; to disability glare, which is so strong that it hinders visual performance.

Sparkle is a small brilliance of light used to add visual interest to objects in a space and to attract attention. Glare results if the area of sparkle is too big, if the source is too bright, or if adjacent reflective surfaces are mirrorlike. The angle, intensity and shielding of the source must be personally evaluated to assure visual comfort.

Lighting professionals often mistakenly attribute glare to the fixture rather than the application. As with all things in life, each situation should be considered in context. A blue sky sets off a fiery sun, making it appear too bright, whereas on a cloudy day, the contrast between sun and sky is reduced, and therefore the sun, while as bright as always, appears less bright—less glary. It's all about contrast and the context within which you view the stimulus. The same principle applies to a light source, such as a reflector lamp. When mounted against a black ceiling in a restaurant, you may pass by it and go, "Ouch." Yet against a light or white ceiling, the effect would be greatly reduced. There are several incremental steps from comfort—or attractive, to discomfort—or offensive, if we were to scale them (see Figure A1-1).

Contrast, context and an individual's sensitivity and cultural preferences will contribute to his or her tolerance of, or receptiveness to, glare. There are times when glare is even desired and can actually be stimulating. Think about it: When you shop at Wal-Mart, where a bright environment is expected, glare may not be distasteful or even noticed; it becomes part of the personality of the store. When you're in Tiffany's, however, you wouldn't expect a generally bright ambiance, but lots of sparkle on the diamonds. Plan your glare.

Attractive   Light Source/Stimulus   Offensive

Figure A1-1. Glare is part of every lighted environment and can be rated on a scale from "attractive" to "offensive." By properly applying it, the designer can influence perception of a space.

Glare can be considered a design adjustment tool. First, determine the appropriate quantity of light source stimulus: When you look at it, is it too much or too little stimulus? It can be visually measured; you know it when you see it in the context of the scene.

When lighting for buildings ...

- *Architectural lighting components* include windows, clerestories, lunettes, skylights, coves, valances, etc. — all integral parts of the structure.
- *Decorative lighting components* include chandeliers, sconces, torchières, lamps, candelabra, etc. —elements that are placed within or attached to the structure.
- *Supplementary lighting components* include downlights, wall washers, accentlights, troffers, etc. —sources of supplementary illumination when the architectural and decorative lighting of the space requires additional illumination.

Source—distribution—location

The basic elements are used to solve lighting problems: What light source is needed? What is its light distribution? What basic equipment and where should it be placed to get the distribution, intensity and properties likely to work best for a particular site?

Equipment should be appropriate for the appearance of decorative elements to ensure it is well-suited to the space. *There are no bad products, only bad applications.* The moment you attach a descriptor of quality to a product, you have exhibited prejudice and limited your ability to make good judgments about design. There are no adverbs or adjectives that have universal approval or disapproval over the infinite spectrum of human appreciation in which this equipment can be used in application. When you assign any characteristic to a product, you have limited your vocabulary of design alternatives in creating a lighting solution. When you hear such praise or pejorative talk about any product, it should be immediately applied as a negative measure upon those who are uttering them.

Any description of equipment not made in context with a very specific application is invalid. It is the highest form of prejudice and, to some extent, exhibits a limited possession of a good design process and ability to see. Keep an open mind. This is where your shield of skepticism should instinctively protect you. Your curiosity can then proceed to track down the truth.

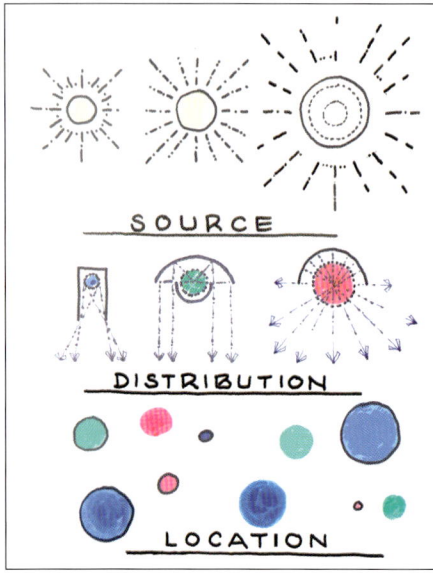

Which characteristics should the source have? How intense, what spectrum, which correlated color temperature, how large?

How much area do you want the source to cover?

Where will you place the source?

Figure A1-2. The three basic elements of lighting: source, distribution and location.

Light is an invisible energy (still undefined) which becomes apparent only when its beam is interrupted by an object.

When we switch all that water to the octave of the electromagnetic spectrum our eyes respond to, we have light. It's there, but you cannot see it—that is, unless you make some smoke, or there is something for the energy to reflect

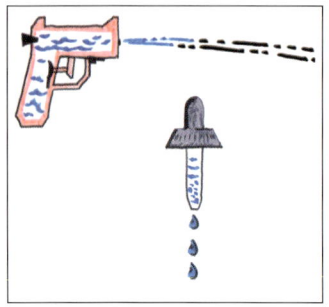

Figure A1-3. Distribution—soft: gentle drops or sharp: directional drops.

Figure A1-4. Distribution: wide/flood; narrow/spot.

LEARNING TO SEE: A Matter of Light

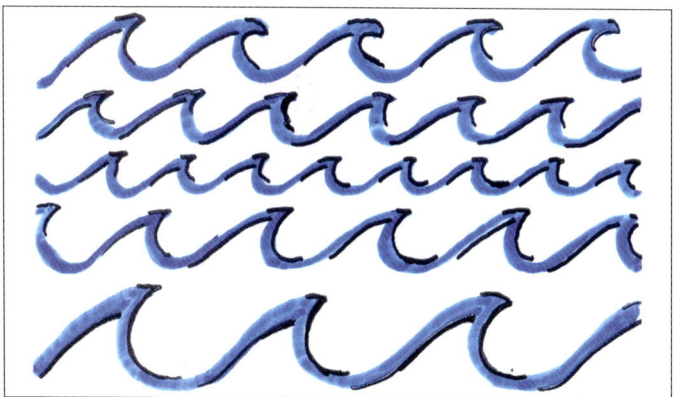

Figure A1-5. **Like water waves—light waves.**

from, or peer at the source itself. Light is truly cerebral. It is transported by our eyes and vision system to be interpreted and evaluated in our brain, tempered by the experiences within our memories.

Distribution of light sources is commonly represented graphically or numerically using a candlepower distribution curve (see Figure A1-6). Candlepower measurements are recorded at several angles around a light source or light fixture, and then plotted in graph form on polar coordinates, resembling a sphere. The distance from the center to any point on the curve gives the candlepower of the source in that direction. When the candlepower distribution is symmetrical around an axis, the lumen output of the source can be derived from an average candlepower distribution curve. The curve is divided into equal zones of 10 degrees each; zonal, or lumen, constants are numerical factors that convert the average candlepower at each zone to the number of lumens in the zone. Equal angular zones on the surface of an imaginary sphere are much greater in areas near the equator than near the poles, therefore a given candlepower produces many more lumens at an angle near the center of the curve than at an angle near the top or the bottom. The zonal lumen factors are based on the relative areas of these angular zones, and their sum from 0° to 180° is 4π or 12.57. A source emitting one candle uniformly in all directions would produce a total of 12.57 lumens. What this means is that two light fixtures that produce exactly the same number of lumens may have very different distributions, and their candlepower curves will have very different shapes and areas.

Direct, semi-direct, general diffuse classifications of light fixtures indicate the distribution of the light between the lower and upper hemispheres. For this reason, the sum of the lumens below 90° and above 90° are expressed as percentages of the sum of the total lumens from 0° to 180°. *Light fixture efficiency* is the ratio of the total lumens emitted by the light fixture to the total lumens generated by the bare lamp.

LUMEN CONSTANTS For Ten-Degree Annular Zones				
Zone	Mid-Zone Angle	Zone	Mid-Zone Angle	Lumen Constant
0°–10°	5°	170°–180°	175°	0.095
10°–20°	15°	160°–170°	165°	0.283
20°–30°	25°	150°–160°	155°	0.463
30°–40°	35°	140°–150°	145°	0.628
40°–50°	45°	130°–140°	135°	0.774
50°–60°	55°	120°–130°	125°	0.897
60°–70°	65°	110°–120°	115°	0.993
70°–80°	75°	100°–110°	105°	1.058
80°–90°	85°	90°–100°	95°	1.091

Figure A1-6.
From Westinghouse *Lighting Handbook*.
ILLUSTRATION BY THE AUTHOR.

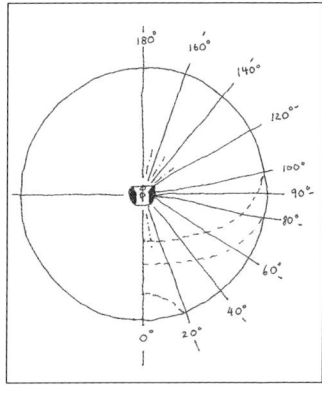

This light fixture in Figure A1-7 shows there are 479 lumens below the horizontal (0°–90°) and 4,563 lumens above, meaning that in the lower hemisphere the light fixture emits 8 percent (479/6,000) of the lumens produced by the bare lamp, and in the upper hemisphere, 76 percent (4,563/6,000) of the bare lamp lumens. The sum of these two percentages, or the ratio of the total lumens produced by the fixture to the lumen output of the bare lamp (5,042/6,000), gives a fixture efficiency of 84 percent. We can determine how the light fixture distributes its light between the two hemispheres by dividing the sums of the lumens below 90° and above 90° by the total fixture lumens: 479/5,042 = 9.5 percent, 4,563/5,042 = 90.5 percent. This fixture qualifies as "indirect" because it directs 9.5 percent of its light below the horizontal and 90.5 percent above.

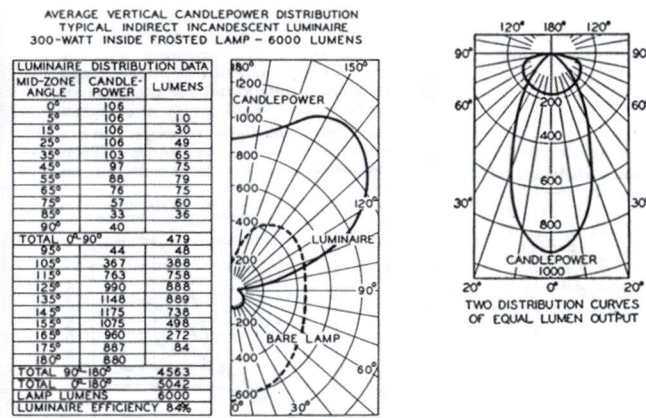

Figure A1-7. **Chart and candlepower distribution curves.**

FROM WESTINGHOUSE *LIGHTING HANDBOOK*.

The Relative Visual Performance (RVP) model

Threshold visual performance deals with what can just be seen. Suprathreshold visual performance is concerned with tasks that are visible because their important aspects are well above threshold levels. This raises the question as to why lighting conditions make a difference to task performance once what has to be seen is visible. The answer is that although the stimuli are visible, lighting influences the speed and accuracy with which the visual information extracted from the stimuli can be processed. Like threshold visual performance, suprathreshold visual performance is governed by such parameters as retinal illuminance, task contrast, visual size and the characteristics of the visual system. Retinal illuminance is largely determined by the luminance of the visual field that is viewed and hence by the illuminance on the surfaces that form that field.

Several studies have been conducted to show how illuminance affects performance, ultimately showing that changing the size and luminance contrast of the target often had a much larger effect on suprathreshold visual performance than increasing the illuminance over any practical range.

The Relative Visual Performance (RVP) model of visual performance (Boyce, P.R. and M.S. Rea, Plateau and escarpment:

The shape of visual performance. *Proceedings: 21st session, Commission Internationale de l'Eclairage.* Paris: Bureau Central de la CIE, 1987) is a quantitative model based on an extensive dataset made up of the changes that occur in reaction time for the detection of visual stimuli seen by the fovea, the central 2° of the retina. This model separated visual from non-visual components by basing the model on simple reaction time—by basing the model on the difference in reaction time that occurs for different combinations of adaptation as a measure.

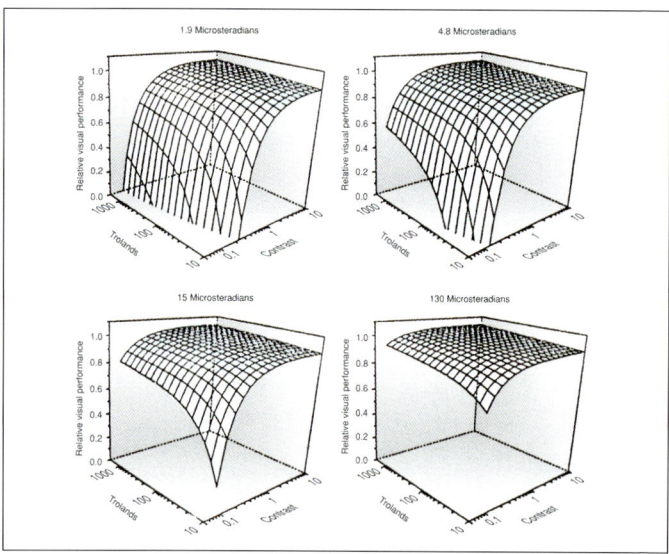

Figure A1-8. **Relative visual performance (RVP) plotted as a function of task contrast and retinal illuminance (in trolands) for several different target sizes measured as solid angle (microsteradians).**

FROM THE IESNA LIGHTING HANDBOOK, 9TH EDITION.

Iluminating measures

Some simple calculation examples:

To get a sense of the general "glow" in a room, what we'll call "Room Glow," divide the total lumens by the total area (floor x ceilings x walls):

$$\frac{TL}{A} = \frac{Total\ Lumens}{Area}$$

Illuminance is the amount of light incident on a surface, measured in lumens per square foot or footcandles (fc) (English unit) or lumens per square meter or lux (lx) (metric unit).

Luminance is the amount of light reflected off a surface in a given direction and measured in candela per square meter (cd/m2) (metric unit).

For example, in a 20' x 20' room, using four light fixtures with one 32-watt fluorescent lamp each (efficacy of 80 lumens/watt), we can calculate:

$$\frac{4 \times 32 \times 80}{400 \text{ sq ft}} = 26 \text{ fc}$$

Typically, most of the illuminance will fall on the horizontal plane, then the ceiling, with the least amount reaching the walls; this will help you figure out how much more light you'll need in different areas of the room.

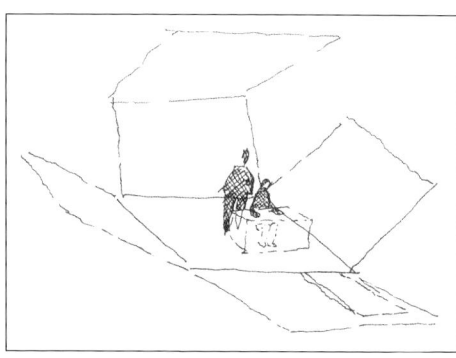

Figure A1-9.
A room can be depicted as an open face Origami, walls and ceiling splayed.

Practice the exercise of:
- guess;
- estimate; and
- measure

in both a darkened room and a lighted room. Understand that the *materials* are the light.

Source data

SOURCE EFFICACY (LUMENS PER WATT)		E = FC per W with LLF
INCANDESCENT	15 - 18 (2 0)	5 - 8
FLUORESCENT	6 0 - 8 0	3 0 - 4 0
H. I. D.	8 0 - 1 0 0	4 0 - 5 0

Illumination approximation equations

$$E = \frac{\text{TOTAL LUMENS} \times \text{CU or EFFICIENCY} \times \text{LLF}}{\text{AREA}}$$

$$\text{TOTAL LUMENS} = \frac{\text{FC} \times \text{AREA}}{(\text{EFF or CU}) \times \text{LLF}}$$

CU or EFF × LLF = .5 - - - INVERSE = 1 / .5 = 2

FIXTURE LUMENS FROM DATA SHEETS (FL) = E_n (RCR) = SPACING

$$\frac{\text{FL} \times .5}{\text{WATTS}} \quad E_{(F)} \text{ PER WATT } \phi$$

VERTICAL E (ILLUMINATION) ESTIMATE

$$\frac{\phi \times E}{\cancel{\angle} \text{ FIXTURE} \times \cos^2 \cancel{\angle} \times \sin \cancel{\angle} \times \text{LLF}} = \text{TOTAL LUMENS REQUIRED}$$

$$\frac{\text{TOTAL LUMENS}}{\text{LAMP LUMENS}} = \text{NUMBER OF FIXTURES REQUIRED}$$

E = ILLUMINATION		
ϕ = SQUARE FOOT		
CU = COEFFICIENT OF UTILIZATION		
FC = FOOTCANDLES		
LLF = LIGHT LOSS FACTOR		
H = HEIGHT ABOVE WORKING SURFACE		

Appendix II
Ethics and Design

> *"Color can distract us from seeing*
> *Sound can distract us from hearing*
> *Flavor can numb our taste"*
> —J. Bruce Burke,
> The Tao of Teaching, 1999

To which we can add…

> *"Codes and standards can distract us from lighting practice."*
> —the author

Energy ethics: Band-aid or cure?

Code or no code, any project design that does not meet the needs of the user is an unethical solution. I always find it ironic that policy makers try to reduce energy use by decreeing the use of less lighting or, more crudely, fewer watts per square foot, rather than addressing the real issue—the promotion of better lighting. Good lighting is inherently energy-ethical.

In the late 1970s, I wrote:
Artificial lighting practice is now reentering an atmosphere of reasonability after its recent excursion towards the outer

limits of energy consumption for lighting measured mostly in terms of radiant energy... In the 1950s, the lighting industry directed and accelerated its course toward a philosophy of "more is better" and "most is best." As a result of this astronomical approach, recommended illuminance levels zoomed to "supernova status with the speed of the rockets that sent our astronauts to the moon."

In 1980, I wrote:
In the future, as in the past, what we do with light will be more significant than how we do it. New source or light fixture technology and design methods continue to be less important than the ends to which they are directed. Until recently, illuminance recommendations told us to use less. The directional thrust of these criteria, as well as their reversal, has little to do with rationality, creativity or humanity. Criteria for lighting appear to respond to the politics of energy. There seems to be a Political Energy Law: lighting consumes energy; therefore, when energy is abundant, use may increase, and when energy is scarce use must be rationed. Please notice that human visual requirements are not a part of this "Political Energy Law."

Obviously I've had opinions on policy. The fluctuating state of energy reserves in this country has done more damage to lighting practice than any other historical event. A

Table A2-1. **Evolution of recommended light levels (footcandles, x 10 to approximate lux) and associated watts per square foot for typical offices).**

Year	IES-recommended minimum light level (average for years 1981 + 1990)	Watts per square foot
1913	2	0.5
1936	10	0.83
1949	30	2.73
1966	45	4.1
1972	70	5.47
1981	40	2.53
1990	32.5	1.53

SOURCE: MIDWEST ENERGY EFFICIENCY ALLIANCE.

glance at the IESNA's illuminance recommendations from the 3rd edition to the 6th edition will show how they have risen and fallen with the energy tide (see Table A2-1).

The pitfalls are always ahead of us. We had better purposefully use enough of the right light to see them. So, do more than follow handbooks—look, see and evaluate! As designers we must rely on our own eyes, brains and hearts, as well as recommendations to be energy ethical, not only with lighting, but with all the resources on our planet.

If you don't practice ethics, there's no virtue in what you do.

Appendix III
Wit and Wisdom

"There are no answers, only musings."
—the author

A lighting designer has to have a holistic view of the job. All jobs are only subsystems of a larger project—an office is a subsystem of a building, and getting to that office, through the lobby and hallways, is all part of that system.

It's a mistake for designers to see something in a magazine and say, "Let's try that"—it may be very wrong for their own application. Designers should start at the beginning with an open mind, looking at all new light sources as a potential for benefit, but not as a benefit for all designs.

You know all is well when thoughtfulness has become instinctive.

Let your mind out of the closet—expose yourself to other people's views. Share those views. Remember, yours are not the only opinions that count.

The problem with lighting designers is that they have become specialists.

Practice and experiment make better theories.

The mark of a good designer is to mock everything up beforehand, knowing then what he's going to get, so there are no surprises, and he can tell his client exactly how the project is going to look. Budget and design are synonymous; don't promote the Taj Mahal and give the client a shack.

The search for the Holy Grail and the "Crusade" created many legendary heroes. The same search has been on in the last quarter of the 20th-century. Today, we call it energy conservation. Few legends will be created.

Be responsible, acquire knowledge through experience, assume the burden of making subjective judgments, do it with comfort.

The speed at which all professionals are forced to work today severely limits the time which they spend together in collaboration. And rarely do they get the opportunity to gain benefit from the diverse peoples who may have great understanding of their current project type and could contribute untold inspiration. This is essentially a removal from the broad contextual stimulation many projects require. These restrictions result in sterile or lesser solutions than would otherwise have been achieved. This is, essentially, the instant suppression of creativity.

In a designer's work for a client, about 40 percent of the value is the preliminary study, the next 40 percent is how tightly I write the spec and guard it. We fight to the death to keep our specs. After 20 years, people know this. When you allow a substitution, you don't get the value difference back to the client.

I am worried that we try to teach students too much instead of arousing their curiosity to learn for themselves. We should only guide them along the paths of knowledge seeking and stop training them.

We must be careful not to subjugate our soul when trying to be analytical.

If we consider some piece of research to be useful, it would be a good idea to plan how to get its usefulness utilized when the work commences.

When two parties disagree, the function of the third party (mediator) is to get them to agree on a solution and not force one upon them.

Lighting consumes very little of our country's primary energy. The main reason to limit the power for lighting is not to save energy, but to reduce the pollution that results from the generation of the power. When we have "clean electricity," we can go back to doing good lighting.

The speed at which you admit to not knowing something lends credibility to any statement you might make about your undertaking the task to find out.

Freedom is the feeling that you can do anything you wish that does no harm to anyone else. Freedom is having that simple discretion of choice for yourself. Any infringement to pander to anyone else's way of life is a limitation of freedom.

Standard practice is for those who are unwilling to assume the burden of finding out what is required. Technology is a tool, standard practice a crutch. What is needed is accountability in design—a burdensome process.

Teaching is the greatest of all design challenges—you are measured by the work of your students.

Argument is the root of knowledge. No discourse can be too rigorous in the pursuit of knowledge!

The real metric of lighting quality is that it makes the user happy.

Creativity, innovation, invention cannot be measured by prescription because it is something that has never been seen before. That old saw that states, "There is nothing new under the sun" is correct. Finding something that already exists in the world is not creating something new—for example, Columbus only bumped into North America, he did not make it. You must make a new thing!

Lighting is the modern pathway to our culture and its preservation.

Light is a promoter, an appreciator, an advancer of our culture.

Learning is forever, training becomes obsolete.

Rules in lighting are a detriment to inspiration.

If you are not advancing the art, you are going backwards.

The basic questions when considering either research or design are: Who cares? Who benefits? Who will buy it?

Design is the key to success in doing anything. The only constant is change.

Never, never, never do anything in moderation; you will lead a boring life.

If my work is not beyond good, I consider it a disaster.

My job is to get it done, not to do it.

To think "outside the box" you first have to know what's in it.

Happiness in lighting is the refinement of the customer's expectations to meet their needs and then delivering that.

About Howard Brandston

HOWARD M. BRANDSTON studied theatrical illumination at Brooklyn College and began his career in lighting in the New York theatre. Prior to founding his own firm in 1966, he was a designer at several manufacturing and lighting design firms, including Century Lighting, Inc., where he served as assistant to Stanley McCandless, one of the pioneer figures in lighting design.

He has more than 50 years of experience in lighting design, engineering and electronics, designing illumination for more than 2,500 commercial, institutional, residential and government projects.

Mr. Brandston received two major awards in 1999. For his contributions to architecture, he was awarded the AIA Institute Honors award. In addition, for his outstanding leadership in the lighting industry, he received the Illuminating Engineering Society Medal, its highest honor—he is the just the fourth designer to be so recognized by the IESNA. In 1992, he was included in the Interior Design Hall of Fame, the only lighting designer ever to be awarded this honor. Mr. Brandston was further honored as an initial inductee of the Lighting Design Hall of Fame and also received the International Association of Lighting Designers Lifetime Achievement Award. In 2006, Mr. Brandston received the IES Louis B. Marks award for Exceptional Service to the

Society. He is one of six people in the 100-year history of the IESNA who has received all of its highest awards. Also in 2006, the Richard Kelly Award was presented to Mr. Brandston for his outstanding contributions to education.

Mr. Brandston is a past president of the IESNA and has addressed forums of the IESNA, the American Institute of Architects, the Institute of Electrical and Electronic Engineers, the Producers Council, the United States Institute of Theatre Technology and others.

He has been a guest lecturer or visiting professor at Ohio University, City College of New York, Cooper Union, Temple University, Hofstra University, Washington University and other institutions. He was Adjunct Professor of Architecture at Rensselaer Polytechnic Institute, where he worked at the Lighting Research Center. He held the Feltman Chair in Lighting at Cooper Union and was adjunct professor of Social Science and Humanities.

His light sculptures have been shown in art galleries throughout the United States and are permanently installed in museums and university collections.

Articles by Mr. Brandston have been published in more than 70 publications, including *Lighting Design + Application, Illuminate,* the Sight Saving Review, *Progressive Architecture* and *Architectural Lighting,* for which he serves as a contributing editor.

He has served on committees for the National Academy of Sciences, and was IESNA's representative to the Architectural and Engineering Federal Energy Committee during the Energy Crisis. His work on energy conservation helped set the initial standards for lighting from 1975 to 1985. He was one of the founding members of the Ad Hoc Committee of Lighting Research and Education Funding Entities, the Lighting Research and Education Fund, the Lighting Research Institute and The Lighting Research Center.

Mr. Brandston is a member of many organizations, including the Architectural League of New York, the Municipal Arts Society, the IESNA, the International Association of Lighting Designers and Britain's Chartered Institute of Building Services Engineers, where he is an Honorary Fellow, an honor limited to 25 living persons.

UNIVERSITY OF ST. THOMAS LIBRARIES

DATE DUE